THE MASTER AND THE DISCIPLE

THE MASTER AND THE DISCIPLE

Interactions between Gandhi and Nehru and their Impact on Modern Indian History

Edited and with an Introduction by

SANGITA MALLIK

Foreword by

BIMAL PRASAD

Under the Auspices of
Rajendra Prasad Academy

MANOHAR
2025

First published 2010
Reprinted 2023, 2025

ISBN 978-81-7304-896-8

Published by
Ajay Kumar Jain *for*
Manohar Publishers & Distributors
4753/23 Ansari Road, Daryaganj
New Delhi 110 002

Typeset by
Kohli Print
Delhi 110 051

Printed at
Replika Press Pvt. Ltd.

Contents

PART TWO

APPENDICES

Foreword

Books on Gandhi have been appearing almost every year. In most of them, however, the writers are paying attention to Gandhi's moral leadership and aspects of his rich personality. Few pay attention to his qualities as a political leader. It is now seldom realized that Gandhi was a unique political leader. One of the key aspects of his success as a political leader was his selection of lieutenants for particular assignments and providing adequate training to them to enable them to do their assigned jobs satisfactorily. His relationship with Nehru specially brings to light this quality of leadership in Gandhi. The impact of that training on Nehru is also well brought out in the Introduction written by the Editor. The result is a book which will be found useful by all those interested in the study of modern Indian history, with particular reference to Gandhi's qualities as a political leader. I heartily congratulate Sangita Mallik for producting this excellent work.

Rajendra Prasad Academy,
New Delhi

BIMAL PRASAD

Introduction

While it is generally known that Mahatma Gandhi had great affection for Jawaharlal Nehru and that this was one of the most important factors in the latter succeeding him as the leading figure in the Indian National Congress and becoming the Prime Minister of India, it is seldom realized that the relationship between the two was one of the determining factors in the history of the Congress and consequently in that of modern India, both before and after the achievement of Independence. To bring all this into focus has been the main objective before me in preparing this work.

I

As is well known, Gandhi was already firmly established as a national hero in the eyes of the overwhelming majority of the Indian people before he landed on Indian soil in 1915 after his long sojourn in South Africa. This was because of his marvellous leadership of the people of Indian origin in South Africa for the removal of their grievances from 1906 onwards. He, on his part, was convinced that the method of that struggle, generally known as satyagraha and based on truth and non-violence, was best suited to be applied by India in the struggle for freedom. The main constituents of satyagraha were non-cooperation and civil disobedience.

Gandhi tested that method first in 1917 in Champaran (Bihar) where he led the fight for the removal of the grievances of peasants against the atrocities of the indigo planters. This was followed in 1918 by his leadership of the struggle of industrial workers at Ahmedabad and that of peasants in

Kheda district in Gujarat. The enactment of the Rowlatt Bill into Act in 1919 gave him an opportunity to apply his technique of struggle on an all-India scale. For the whole country was quite upset by that Act.

During the First World War (1914–18) the Indian people had by and large supported the British side in it. Gandhi also had taken an enthusiastic part in urging the Indian people to offer themselves as recruits for service in the British Indian Army. However, he had made clear to the British that he was following that policy in the hope that it would lead India sooner to swaraj. When, however, the war ended, repression took precedence over reforms at the hands of the British. Gandhi, along with six of his close friends, gave a call for a nation-wide movement on 6 April 1919 involving defiance of the Rowlatt Act. This was something new in India's history and had an electrifying impact on the mind of Jawaharlal, then thirty and practicing as a barrister at Allahabad under the supervision of his father, Motilal Nehru, an eminent lawyer as well as one of the prominent leaders of the Congress. This is best reflected in the following lines written by him in his classic, *The Discovery of India*, first published in 1946:

> And then Gandhi came. He was like a powerful current of fresh air that made us stretch ourselves and take deep breaths; like a beam of light that pierced the darkness and removed the scales from our eyes; like a whirlwind that upset many things, but most of all the working of people's minds. He did not descend from the top; he seemed to have emerged from the millions of India, speaking their language, and incessantly drawing attention to them and their appalling condition. . . . The essence of his teaching was fearlessness and truth, and action allied to these, always keeping the welfare of the masses in view.

Beginning with 1919, which marked the beginning of the Age of Gandhi in Indian history, Jawaharlal became a devoted follower of Gandhi. This became a great asset for

Gandhi, for the former, at once emerged as a darling of the educated youth of India. Besides, it was primarily because of his young disciple that Gandhi was able to enlist the active support of Motilal Nehru. The latter was at first quite sceptic about the efficacy of Gandhi's method of struggle for winning freedom. However, with his deep love for his only son, who was preparing to go to prison as a soldier of Gandhi, he could not imagine to keep himself out of the struggle. So he became the first senior leader of the Congress to join Gandhi, thus adding significantly to the latter's prestige.

II

The beginning of 1926–7 marked a new phase in Jawaharlal's life and thought and consequently also in his relationship with Gandhi. By the time the former returned to India in December 1927 after a long sojourn in Western Europe and a much shorter one in the Soviet Union he came endowed with a new vision. While in Western Europe he had actively participated in the anti-imperialist conference at Brussels in February 1927 as a representative of the Indian National Congress and had been elected a member of its presidium. When the Conference set up a worldwide organization called the League against Imperialism, Jawaharlal was elected as one of the presidents of its Council, the others being Albert Einstein, Romain Rolland, Madam Sun Yat Sen and George Lansbury. The Communists had played a major role in that venture and the contact with them turned Nehru into a radical and a socialist. Although remaining loyal to Gandhi he no longer felt circumscribed by the latter's vision and become eager to move forward in both political and socio-economic spheres. As he puts it in his *Autobiography*, first published in 1936:

My outlook was wider, and nationalism by itself seemed to me definitely a narrow and insufficient creed. Political freedom, independence, were no doubt essential, but they were steps only in the right direction. Without social freedom and a socialist structure of society and the State, neither the country nor the individual could develop much. I felt I had a clearer perception of world affairs, more grip on the present-day world, ever changing as it was.

The proceedings of the annual session of the Congress held in the last week of December 1927 bear ample proof of Nehru's new outlook. He presented a number of resolutions—on independence, war danger, the League against Imperialism, etc. All the resolutions he moved were adopted without much discussion. The Master, however, was not happy with the performance of his disciple. He was particularly irked by the resolution declaring that the goal of the Congress was the achievement of national independence. Although the goal as defined in the Congress constitution—the achievement of swaraj, which could mean either independence or Dominion Status, depending on circumstances, remained intact, Gandhi was not at all happy with the new resolution. He wrote to Nehru on 4 January 1928:

You are going too fast. You should have taken time to think and become acclimatized. Most of the resolutions you framed and got carried could have been delayed for one year. Your plunging into the 'republican army' was a hasty step.

This was followed by another letter in which Gandhi chastized Jawaharlal in more severe terms, charging him with having turned the Congress into 'a school boys' debating society'. This drew from Nehru quite an angry reply in which he strongly criticized Gandhi's style of functioning since his release from prison in 1924 and his failure to provide satisfactory leadership to people who were still looking towards him for it. Gandhi now lost patience. He wrote to Nehru on 17 January 1928:

> If any freedom is required from me, I give you all the freedom you may need from the humble, unquestioning allegiance that you have given to me for all those years. . . . I see clearly that you must carry on open warfare against me and my views. . . . The differences between you and me appear to me be so vast and radical that there seems to be no meeting ground between us.

That implied parting between them as political comrades. Gandhi did not stop there and proceeded to put that implication in black and white. For he added:

> I can't conceal my grief that I should lose a comrade so valiant, so faithful, so able and so honest as you have always been; but in serving a cause comradeships have got to be sacrificed. The cause must be held superior to all such considerations. But this dissolution of comradeship, if dissolution must come, in no way affects our personal intimacy. We have long become members of the same family and we remain such in spite of grave political differences.

Nehru immediately sent a reply which had a soothing impact on his relationship with Gandhi. The full text is given in Chapter 4 and only a few lines need be cited here:

> Your letter came as a bit of a shock and was painful reading. Painful because with relentless logic you have contemplated certain eventualities which I had not considered possible or even thought of in their entirety. . . . Is any assurance from me necessary that nothing that can ever happen can alter or lessen my deep regard and affection for you? That regard and affection is certainly personal, but it is something more. No one had moved me and inspired me more than you and I can never forget your exceeding kindness for me. There can be no question of our personal relations suffering. But seen in the wider sphere am I not your child in politics, though perhaps a truant and errant child ?

III

Gandhi now realized that he had gone a bit too far and the Disciple remained a true disciple. The relations between the two were back to where they were till 1927. This is well illustrated by the telegram Gandhi sent to Jawaharlal on his performance in leading a Congress procession at Lucknow, with strict adherence to non-violence, in spite of extreme provocation by the police, as a part of the all-India campaign against the Simon Commission. In his letter to Nehru dated 3 December 1928 Gandhi observed:

> My love to you. It was all done bravely. You have greater things to do. May God spare you for many a long year to come and make you His chosen instrument for freeing India from foreign yoke.

In 1929 as a result chiefly of Gandhi's insistence, Nehru, then forty, though initially reluctant to take the burden, was elected President of the Congress. Jawaharlal initially wanted Gandhi himself to be president. The final decision in this regard was taken at a meeting of the All India Congress Committee in September 1929. Ten Provincial Congress Committees had proposed Gandhi's name, five of Vallabhbhai Patel, who had begun to be called Sardar Patel because of his able leadership of the struggle of peasants against enhancement of rent at Bardoli (Gujarat) in 1928, and only three for Jawaharlal. However, Gandhi's view prevailed and Jawaharlal was unanimously elected President. What Gandhi said about Jawaharlal on that occasion while proposing his name is worth citing:

> In bravery he is not to be surpassed. Who can excel him in the love of the country? 'He is rash and impetuous', say some. This quality is an additional qualification at the present moment. And if he has the dash and rashness of a warrior, he has also the prudence of a statesman. A lover

of discipline, he has shown himself capable of rigidly submitting to it even when it has seemed irksome. He is undoubtedly an extremist, thinking far ahead of his surroundings. But he is humble and practical enough not to force the pace to the breaking point. He is pure as the crystal, he is truthful beyond suspicion. . . . The nation is safe in his hands.

As is well known, the Congress session in December 1929, held at Lahore, at which Jawaharlal presided, forms a landmark in our history. It was at that session that complete independence was declared as the goal of the Congress and this became a part of the Congress constitution. Jawaharlal unfurled the flag of independence and declared in his presidential address that he was a republican and a socialist.

IV

Although not so powerful in the Congress organization, with his growing popularity among the masses as well as the intelligentsia and the youth and the strong patronage of Gandhi Jawaharlal now began to emerge more and more as the political heir to Gandhi. The latter also came to that conclusion in spite of sharp differences with Nehru on several occasions as illustrated by the exchange of letters between the two in the 1930s included in this selection. Thus in 1934 in a letter to no less a person than Sardar Patel, Gandhi observed that in his opinion Jawaharlal was likely to be the 'future helmsman of the Congress'. Gandhi soon made his thinking on that issue known to Nehru himself and began to train him for achieving that position. In 1936 when at Gandhi's suggestion Nehru was elected President of the Congress for the second time, he felt very uncomfortable in the company of the old leaders headed by Sardar Patel and Rajendra Prasad who formed a majority in the Congress

Working Committee. He felt so unhappy because of it that he wrote to Gandhi complaining about the attitude of the old leaders who were always filling the various sub-committees formed from time to time with their own followers. Besides, Rajendra Prasad had sent a letter to him on behalf of the old leaders of the Congress mentioning that he was ruining the Congress by his speeches during his tours in the country. For he was most of the time talking about socialism which had not been adopted as a goal of the Congress. Gandhi's reply to Nehru's complaint illustrates how he was training the latter for leadership:

> Why do you resent their [the old leaders'] majority being reflected in all the sub-committees etc.? Is it not the most natural thing? You are in office, by their unanimous choice but you are not in power yet. To put you in office was an attempt to find you in power quicker then you would otherwise have been. Any way, that was at the back of my mind when I suggested your name for the crown of thorns. Keep it on, though the head be bruised.

Gandhi at the same time informed Nehru that he had instructed his secretary, Mahadev Desai, to ensure that no one else should have access to their correspondence. What could be more assuring to the Disciple than this that he was being assiduously trained by the Master for acquiring the supreme position in the Congress?

In 1946 when it became clear that the person who held the crown in the Congress would also hold the same in the government, Gandhi ensured that the crown of the Congress should be held by Nehru. When Maulana Azad's term as Congress President has ended and someone else had to be elected in his place, nominations were called from Provincial Congress Committees. A majority of the Committees suggested Sardar Patel's name. Not one committee had nominated Nehru's. However, Gandhi emphatically told the members of the Working Committee that in the then prevailing situation in the country, when serious negotiations were likely to be held between the Congress and the representatives of the government, Nehru was the only fit person to become president. As the members of the Working Committee could also nominate a person for presidentship, Gandhi then and there asked J.B. Kripalani, who had been holding the position of General Secretary of the Congress since long, to do the needful and the latter duly filed a nomination for Nehru and this was supported by the entire membership of the Working Committee. Sardar Patel having already supported Gandhiji's suggestion. It goes without saying that it was because of his position as Congress President thus Nehru first became the Vice-President of the Interim Government on 2 September 1946 and later Prime Minister on 15 August 1947 to the delight of the overwhelming majority of the Indian people.

Gandhi, had, of course, prepared the ground for it by publicly declaring at a meeting of the All India Congress Committee in 1941 that he had marked out Nehru as his successor, adding:

> He says that he does not understand my language, and that he speaks in a language foreign to me. But language is no bar to a union of hearts. And I know this that when I am gone, he will speak my language.

In the meanwhile, after going so far to underline that Nehru was his political heir and putting him in a clearly leading position in the Congress, Gandhi had been anxious to find out how far his beloved disciple agreed with him on certain basic issues of policy, particularly in the economic sphere. On 5 October 1945 he wrote to Nehru:

> I take first the sharp difference of opinion that has emerged between us. If such a difference really exists people should also know about it. . . . I have said that I fully stand by the kind of governance which I have described in *Hind Swaraj* [1909]. . . . I believe that if India and through India the world, is to achieve real freedom then sooner or later we shall have to go and live in villages — in huts, not in palaces. Millions of people can never live in cities and palaces in comfort and peace. . . .

Nehru politely but firmly begged to differ. He said in reply that he had read *Hind Swaraj* many years ago and had only a vague picture in his mind. However, he did remember that even then the picture presented seemed to him 'completely unusual'. Nehru further added: 'As you know, the Congress has never considered that picture, much less adopted it'. So the discussion between Gandhi and Nehru resulted in stalemate. Gandhi was able to talk to Nehru about it on 12 November 1945. But his hope they could meet again to further discuss that matter never materialized. The political developments taking place in India during 1945–7 overwhelmed then and they had no time to discuss such fundamental issues as raised by Gandhi in his letter dated 5 October 1945.

However, it is important to note that in spite of his differences with Nehru on economic policy Gandhi, as noted earlier, continued to persist in his endeavour to put Nehru at the top of Congress leadership and consequently as the head of the Government of India when freedom was achieved. As a result, because of the communal carnage taking place in areas surrounding Delhi in the wake of Partition, the bond between Gandhi and Nehru became much stronger than before. When Gandhi undertook a fast to bring about communal harmony in January 1948, Nehru, thought not believing in fasting, could not persuade himself to take food. When ending his fast Gandhi wrote to Nehru on 18 January

1948, exactly twelve days before his assassination by a Hindu fanatic: 'Give up your fast. . . . May you live long and continue to be the jewel of India'. This episode vividly illustrates the deep personal as well as political attachment between Gandhi and Nehru, which had continued for nearly thirty years.

V

This attachment had a significant impact on our history. While Gandhi was throughout the Master and Nehru the Disciple, it is not merely the latter who learnt from the former. They actually influenced each other. Although Nehru generally accepted Gandhi's guidance, the latter also adopted many of the latter's views. Indeed it can be said that as a result of their interactions, there emerged a Gandhi–Nehru synthesis which lay behind many, though not all the important Congress decisions between 1929 and 1947. Thus, as we have noticed earlier, while Gandhi had reprimanded Nehru in January 1928 for pushing the resolution on independence at the Congress session of 1927, he soon came to realize that in that respect Nehru truly represented the views of the educated youth of the country and not only pushed forward his name for the presidentship of the Congress session of 1929 held at Lahore, but himself moved the resolution adopting Complete Independence as the goal of the Congress.

The first five of the Appendices given in this book illustrate the working of the Gandhi–Nehru synthesis in the Congress decisions. The first one giving the text of the resolution on fundamental rights and economic policy, drafted by Nehru and adopted by the Karachi Congress in 1931, is one of the best illustrations of the joint working of the minds of Gandhi and Nehru. The second appendix containing the statement issued by the Congress Working Committee on 14 September 1939, drafted by Nehru, explaining the Congress attitude towards India's role in the Second World War, which had broken out recently, ironically falls in the same category though on a superficial view it illustrates a contradiction between the views of Gandhi and those of Nehru. While Gandhi, after seeing the Viceroy had hoped that the Congress would extend its moral support to Britain in the war without any condition, the resolution of the Working Committee, drafted by Nehru, promised full support to Britain if the latter made it clear that they were fighting for the cause of democracy and freedom, which would be applied to India also. However, Gandhi's comment on that resolution showed that he did not fundamentally disagree with the latter. For he strongly commended Nehru for drafting that resolution and appealed to the British government to accept the demand contained in it.

The third and fourth appendices illustrate how Gandhi and Nehru reconciled their views at a critical time in the history of the Indian struggle for freedom and worked out a synthesis which became the basis of Congress policy in 1942 and formed the ideological background of the famous Quit India movement. After the failure of the negotiations with the Cripps Mission in March 1942, Gandhi came to the conclusion that the only solution to the Indian problem was for the British to quit India immediately. If they did not comply with that suggestion, the Congress should launch a non-violent mass movement to force them to do so. Nehru was strongly approved to Gandhi's new move. His sympathies were on the side of Britain and her chief allies, including China, the Soviet Union and the United States of America and did not want the Congress to adopt Gandhi's policy at a time when the latter were facing a critical situation in the war. He was particularly concerned with the plight of China and the Soviet Union and did not want anything to be done which might weaken their position. He was also hopeful that the United States might bring pressure on Britain to agree to transfer power to Indian hands with a view to ensuring the victory of the United Nations. These arguments failed to satisfy Gandhi and he stuck to his line. However, he realized the importance of having Nehru on his side and more and more he linked his demand for British withdrawal from India with the victory of the United Nations and showed keen concern with the plight of China and the Soviet Union. Nehru, on the other hand, noticed that Gandhi's weakly writings in the *Harijan*, reproduced in all the newspapers in India, had already created a ferment in the country and things were inevitably moving towards a struggle. In such a situation, he could not imagine himself standing away from Gandhi. When the All India Congress Committee met in Bombay on 7 August 1942, it was none else than Nehru who moved the famous Quit India resolution. The resolution itself represented an excellent synthesis of the views of the Master and the Disciple. Appendices 3 and 4 illustrate the main elements of the Gandhi–Nehru synthesis on India's role in world affairs and need not detain us here.

It may be added that a similar synthesis was simultaneously turning the Congress in the direction of socialism. In this respect Nehru was a pioneer, as shown above. However, Gandhi, being deeply concerned with the problem of poverty in India, in line with the old Congress policy, also gradually moved towards socialism in spite of the opposition of the old leaders of the Congress. Although the Congress never accepted socialism as its objective before Independence, a study of its resolutions from 1929 to 1947 will show that thanks to the Gandhi–Nehru synthesis it was steady moving in that direction. The resolution adopted by the All India Congress Committee setting up the Objectives and Economic Programme Committee, adopted on 15 June 1947, and reproduced in Appendix 5 is a good illustration of the progress made by the Congress in its march towards socialism till then as a result of the Gandhi–Nehru synthesis. The composition of the Committee is also indicative of the preparedness of the Congress to accept socialist ideas. Besides Nehru, two prominent socialist leaders, Jayaprakash Narayan and Achyut Patwardhan were also its members.

Appendices 6 to 9 represent some of the most moving speeches and writings of Nehru on Gandhi after the latter's passing away. The speech beginning with the words, 'The Light has gone out', is well known, but there are several other equally moving speeches of Nehru, following that speech, paying tribute to Gandhi and filled with the deepest emotions, which have been included here. These vividly illustrate the deep emotional attachment of Nehru towards Gandhi. Appendix 10 puts together Nehru's reminiscences of Gandhi as put together by him from time to time and latter included in one of the chapters in his book on Gandhi, published after the latter's death.

VI

It remains to point out that the impact of Gandhi–Nehru synthesis was not only confined to Congress before 1947, but also extended to the period after 1947 and continued at least till the passing away of Nehru in May 1964. Firstly, it proved to be a major factor in shaping Nehru's style of leadership as prime minister. He had learnt from the Master the importance of keeping the Congress united as far as possible and not insisting on maintaining one's own line of policy regardless of what other prominent leaders felt. Just as the Congress had been the main instrument in the struggle for Indian freedom, Nehru realized that it functioned as the chief instrument for maintaining India's national unity. He continued to have differences with the older leaders of the Congress like Sardar Patel and Rajendra Prasad, just as earlier, but he never forgot the lesson taught by Gandhi that he should remember that they represented the majority opinion in the Congress organization and should try to work in co-operation with them. The leaders of the Congress Socialist Party were not happy with that policy of Nehru, but the latter knew that they had only a small following inside the Congress and so could afford to ignore them.

This consideration of carrying with him the majority of Congress leaders also led Nehru to modify his socio-economic policies, putting much less emphasis on socialism than he had done in the 1930s. Indeed he began to say during 1947–8 onwards that India's economic problems were not going to be solved by any 'ism', but by larger production. Later on, when he realized by mid-1950s that it was possible to move the Congress in the direction of socialism without bringing about a major split in it, he pushed forward a resolution at the Avadi session of the Congress in 1955 declaring that it would work for building up 'a socialistic' pattern of society in India.

In the field of economic policy while Nehru attached due importance to building up heavy industries, in order to meet the requirements of a modern State, he did not ignore small industries and helped them as far as possible. At the same time, he did not forget Gandhi's teaching that India lived in villages and his government made generous allocations for modernization of agriculture. He did not succeed in ushering in land reforms on a large scale, beyond the abolition of the zamindari system, but lent full support to the Bhoodan movement launched by Vinoba Bhave.

Nehru as prime minister always remained conscious of the fact that he was Gandhi's disciple. The latter had emphasized that as India was fighting for Independence through non-violent means, free India would have a special mission in the world, that being to work for peace and brotherhood among nations. Almost all authorities on India's foreign policy during the Nehru Era (1947–64) are united in the view that Nehru always kept that teaching in view and tried to implement it in practice as far as possible for a prime minister to do so. Indeed, Gandhi's observation in 1941 that Nehru would speak in the formers' language after he was gone, proved literally true at least in respect of foreign policy. Nehru often referred to Gandhi's teachings in his major speeches on India's foreign policy and spoke like his disciple. This is confirmed by what my teacher, Prof. Bimal Prasad, told me once about his experience when he had called upon Nehru to present a copy of his book *The Origins of Indian Foreign Policy* (Calcutta, 1960):

> After Nehru had looked through the index of that book, paying particular attention to the entries under his own name. I showed him the page on dedication in my book. That ran as follows: '*Dedicated to the sacred memory of Mahatma Gandhi, whose teachings form the bed-rock of India's foreign policy and whose voice is still heard by the world through his disciple and political heir*'. When I followed this by asking Nehru whether he approved of that dedication, the latter, without any hesitation, nodded his head in approval.

Thus the Disciple admitted that he was speaking in the language of the Master at any rate when speaking on India's foreign policy, this was no doubt a claim which was fully justified.

In the end, a few words about the sources for the materials

and quotations used in this book. Part One, containing the text of correspondence between Gandhi and Nehru is based on *Collected Works of Mahatma Gandhi* and *Selected Works of Jawaharlal Nehru*, depending on whether the letters are from Gandhi or from Nehru. The letters from Gandhi to Nehru used in the Introduction are based on the chapters in Part One. Other citations are taken from Nehru's *Autobiography* and his *Discovery of India*. Citations from Gandhi's reference to Nehru in his speeches will be found in *Collected Works*. The text of resolutions will be found in the *Proceedings of the Congresss* or the volumes of the *India Quarterly Register*. This method has been followed in order to avoid the use of footnotes.

SANGITA MALLIK

PART ONE

SELECT CORRESPONDENCE BETWEEN GANDHI AND NEHRU

CHAPTER 1

Gandhi to Nehru[1]

Satyagraha Ashram,
Sabarmati
4.1.1928

My Dear Jawaharlal,

I feel that you love me too well to resent what I am about to write. In any case I love you too well to restrain my pen when I feel I must write.

You are going too fast. You should have taken time to think and become acclimatized. Most of the resolutions you framed and got carried could have been delayed for one year. Your plunging into the 'republican army' was a hasty step. But I do not mind these acts of yours so much as I mind your encouraging mischief-makers and hooligans. I do not know whether you still believe in unadulterated non-violence. But even if you have altered your views, you could not think that unlicensed and unbridled violence is going to deliver the country. If careful observation of the country in the light of your European experiences convinces you of the error of the current ways and means, by all means enforce your own views, but do please form a disciplined party. . . .

Yours,
Bapu

[1] *The Collected Works of Mahatma Gandhi* (hereafter cited as *Collected Works M.G.*), Vol. XXXV (New Delhi, 1969), pp. 432–3.

CHAPTER 2

Nehru to Gandhi[1]

Allahabad,
11.01.1928

My dear Bapuji,

. . . . . .

I am loth to inflict another letter on you so soon after my last but I am very much troubled by your criticism of the Congress resolutions and I feel I must write to you again. You are always very careful with your words and your language is studiously restrained. It amazes me all the more to find you using language which appears to me wholly unjustified. You have condemned in general language the proceedings of the Subjects Committee and specially selected some resolutions for greater criticism and condemnation. May I point out that it is always unsafe to judge on hearsay evidence? You were not present yourself and it is quite conceivable that the opinions you may have formed after a personal visit to the Subjects Committee may have been different. Yet you have chosen to condemn and judge unfavourably the whole committee, or at any rate a great majority of it, simply basing your judgement on the impressions of a few persons. Do you think this is quite fair to the committee or the Congress? You have referred to discipline and to the Working Committee as the National Cabinet. May I remind you that you are a mem-

[1] *Selected Works of Jawaharlal Nehru*, ed. S. Gopal (hereafter cited as *Selected Works J.N.*), Vol. 7 (New Delhi, 1975), pp. 371–6 also see *Collected Works M.G.*, Vol. XXXV (New Delhi, 1969), pp. 540–1.

ber of the Working Committee and it is an extraordinary thing for a member, on the morrow of the Congress, to criticize and run down the Congress and its principal resolutions? There has been a general chorus of congratulations on the success of the Madras Congress. This may be wrong or without sufficient basis but undoubtedly there was this general impression in the country and atmosphere counts for a great deal in all public work. And now most people who thought so feel a bit dazed at your criticism and wonder if their previous enthusiasm was not overdone or mistaken.

You have described the independence resolution as 'hastily conceived and thoughtlessly passed'. I have already pointed out to you how the country has discussed and considered this question for years past and how I have personally thought over it, discussed it, spoken about it in meetings, written about it and generally been full of it for the last five yeas or more. It seems to me that under the circumstances no stretch of language can justify the use of the words 'hastily conceived'. As for 'thoughtlessly passed', I wonder if you know that the resolution was discussed in the Subjects Committee for about three hours and more than a dozen speeches for and against were made. Ultimately as you know it was passed almost unanimously both in the committee and the open Congress. Were all the people in the committee and the Congress who voted for it 'thoughtless'? Is this not rather a strange assumption? And why should it not be said with greater truth that the small minority opposed to the resolution were mistaken? You mention that last year the resolution was rejected by the committee. I do not know what inference you draw from this but to me it seems obvious that this can only mean that the committee and the Congress have been eager to pass it in the past as in the present but refrained from doing so out of regard for you. I hope you will agree with me that it is not healthy politics for any organization to subordinate its own definite opinion on a public issue out of personal regard only.

I am not referring here to the merits of the resolution. But I shall only say this that after prolonged and careful thought a demand for independence and all that this implies has come to mean a very great deal for me and I attach more importance to it than to almost anything else. I have thought over every word you said the other day in Madras on this question and it has merely confirmed me in my opinion. But I doubt if anyone outside a small circle understands your position in regard to this. I am sure that none of the others—liberals, etc.—who want Dominion Status think in the same way with you. Yesterday Sir Ali Imam addressed a meeting here on the Simon boycott. I also spoke for a few minutes and like King Charle's head independence cropped up and I laid stress on it. After the meeting Ali Imam told me that I did well in laying stress on this; he and his friends would probably come round to this position sooner or later but for the time being they had to be a little restrained as they wanted to carry many people with them. I am sure most liberals welcome the independence resolution, whatever they may say about it, as they feel that it strengthens their position. But whether they like it or not, it passes my comprehension how a national organization can have as its ideal and goal Dominion Status. The very idea suffocates and strangles me.

I took no special interest in the resolution on the boycott of British goods chiefly because I felt that it would meet with your strong disapproval and the boycott could not success unless a more or less unanimous effort was made. But I have no doubt that it can be made into a partial success if there was some unanimity in our own ranks. You must have read about the wonderful effectiveness of the boycott in China. There was nothing special in China which we have not got and there is no fundamental reason why we cannot succeed where they succeeded. But granting that it is not likely to succeed, is it such a laughing matter after all? Has our boycott of foreign cloth by *khaddar* succeeded so remarkably—has our spinning franchise succeeded? They have not but you did not hesitate to press them on the country and the Congress because you felt, and rightly, that they would be good for this nation even if they did not wholly succeed.

Having singled out two resolutions for your special condemnation you casually refer to the others as 'several irresponsible resolutions'. Excepting the Unity resolution every other resolution of the Congress may come under this heading. And so the labours of the 200 and odd persons in the Subjects Committee and the larger numbers in the Congress are summarily and rather contemptuously disposed of. It is very hard luck on the unhappy persons who, though wanting perhaps in foresight and intelligence did not spare themselves and tried to do their best. We have all 'sunk to the level of the school boys' debating society' and you chastise us like an angry school master, but a school master who will not guide us or give us lessons but will only point out from time to time the error of our ways. Personally I very much wish that we were more like real school boys, with the life and energy and daring of school boys, and a little less like the right honourable gentlemen who are for ever weighting the pros and cons and counting the cost.

You know how intensely I have admired you and believed in you as a leader who can lead this country to victory and freedom. I have done so in spite of the fact that I hardly agreed with anything that some of your previous publications—*Indian Home Rule* (*Hind Swaraj*), etc., contained. I felt and felt that you were and are infinitely greater than your little books. Above everything I admire action and daring and courage and I found them all in you in a superlative degree. And I feel instinctively that however much I may disagree with you, your great personality and your possession of these qualities would carry us to our goal. During the non-cooperation period you were supreme; you were in your element and automatically you took the right step. But since you came out of prison something seems to have gone wrong and you have been very obviously ill at ease. You will remember how within a few months or even weeks you repeatedly changed your attitude—the Juhu statements, the A.I.C.C. meeting at Ahmedabad and after, etc.—and most of us were left in utter bewilderment. That bewilderment has continued since then. I have asked you many times what you expected to do in the future and your answers have been far from satisfying. All you have said has been that within a year or 18 months you expected the *khadi* movement to spread rapidly and in a geometric ratio and then some direct action in the political field might be indulged in several years and 18 months have passed since then and the miracle has not happened. It was difficult to believe that it would happen but faith in your amazing capacity to bring off the improbable kept us in an expectant mood. But such faith for an irreligious person like me is a poor reed to rely on and I am beginning to think if we are to wait for freedom till *khadi* becomes universal in India we shall have to wait till the Greek Kalends. *Khadi* will grow slowly, and if war comes it will grow very fast, but I do not see how freedom is coming in its train. As I mentioned before to you our *khadi* work is almost wholly divorced from politics and our *khadi* workers are developing a mentality which does not concern itself with anything outside their limited sphere of work. This maybe good for the work they do, but little can be expected from them in the political field.

What then can be done? You say nothing. You only criticize and no helpful lead comes from you. You tell us that if the country will not even take to *khadi* how can we expect it to do anything more difficult or daring. I do not think the reasoning is correct. If the country does not go ahead politically by one method, surely it is up to our leaders to think of other or additional methods.

Reading many of your articles in *Young India*—your autobiography, etc. I have often felt how very different my ideals were from yours and I have felt that you were very hasty in your judgements, or rather having arrived at certain conclusions you were over-eager to justify them by any scrap of evidence you might get. I remember how in an article on the 'Two Ways'—or some such title—you gave some newspaper cuttings from America about crime and immorality and contrasted American civilization with India. I felt it was something like Katherine Mayo drawing conclusions from some unsavoury hospital statistics. Your long series of articles based on the French book *Towards Moral Bankruptcy*—also made one feel the same way. You misjudge greatly I think the civilization of the West and attach too great an importance to its many failings. You have stated somewhere that India has nothing to learn from the West and that she has reached a pinnacle of wisdom in the past. I entirely disagree with this viewpoint and I neither think that the so-called *Rama Raj* was very good in the past, nor do I want it back. I think the Western or rather industrial civilization is bound to conquer India, may be with many changes and adaptations, but nonetheless in the main based on industrialism. You have criticized strongly the many obvious defects of industrialism and hardly paid any attention to its merits. Everybody knows these defects and all the utopias and social theories are meant to remove them. It is the opinion of most thinkers in the

West that these defects are not due to industrialism as such but to the capitalist system which is based on exploitation of others. I believe you have stated that in your opinion there is no necessary conflict between Capital and Labour. I think that under the capitalist system this conflict is unavoidable.

You have advocated very eloquently and forcefully the claims of *daridranarayana*—the poor in India. I do believe that the remedy you have suggested is very helpful to them and if adopted by them in large numbers will relieve to some extent their misery. But I doubt very much if the fundamental causes of poverty are touched by it. You do not say a word against the semi-feudal zamindari system which prevails in a great part of India or against the capitalist exploitation of both the workers and the consumers.

But I must stop. I have already exceeded all reasonable limits and I hope you will forgive me. My only excuse is my mental agitation. I did not want to become Secretary of the A.I.C.C., as I wanted perfect freedom to say and do what I considered necessary. But [M.A.] Ansari pressed me on the ground that many of my resolutions and specially the independence resolution, had been passed by the Congress and I thus had full freedom to work on my own lines. I could not answer this argument and had to accept. Now I find that every effort is being made to belittle and ridicule these very Congress resolutions and it is a painful experience.

Yours affectionately,
Jawahar

CHAPTER 3

Gandhi to Nehru[1]

The Ashram,
Sabarmati,
17.01.1928

My Dear Jawaharlal,

. . . . Though I was beginning to detect some differences in viewpoint between you and me, I had no notion whatsoever of the terrible extent of these differences. Whilst you were heroically suppressing yourself for the sake of the nation and in the belief that by working with and under me in spite of yourself, you would serve the nation and come out scatheless, you were chafing under the burden of this unnatural self-suppression. And, while you were in that state, you overlooked the very things which appear to you now as my serious blemishes. I could show you from the pages of *Young India* equally strong articles written by me, when I was actively guiding the Congress with reference to the doings of the All-India Congress Committee. I have spoken similarly at the All-India Congress Committee meetings whenever there has been irresponsible and hasty talk or action. But whilst you were under stupefaction these things did not jar on you as they do now. And it seems to me, therefore, useless to show you the discrepancies in your letter. What I am now concerned with is future action.

If any freedom is required from me, I give you all the free-

[1] *Collected Works M.G.*, Vol. XXXV (New Delhi, 1969), pp. 469–70.

dom you may need from the humble, unquestioning allegiance that you have given to me for all these years and which I value all the more for the knowledge I have now gained of your state. I see quite clearly that you must carry on open warfare against me and my views. For, if I am wrong I am evidently doing irreparable harm to the country and it is your duty after having known it to rise in revolt against me. Or, if you have any doubt as to the correctness of your conclusion, I shall gladly discuss them with you personally. The differences between you and me appear to me to be so vast and radical that there seems to be no meeting-ground between us. I can't conceal from you my grief that I should lose a comrade so valiant, so faithful, so able and so honest as you have always been; but in serving a cause, comradeships have got to be sacrificed. The cause must be held superior to all such considerations. But this dissolution of commandership if dissolution must come—in no way affects our personal intimacy. We have long become members of the same family, and we remain such in spite of grave political differences. I have the good fortune to enjoy such relations with several people. To take [V.S. Srinivas] Shastri for instance, he and I differ in the political outlook as poles asunder, but the bond between him and me that sprung up before we knew the political differences has persisted and survived for fiery ordeals it had to go through.

I suggest a dignified way of unfurling your banner. Write to me a letter for publication showing your differences. I will print it in *Young India* and write a brief reply. Your first letter I destroyed after reading and replying to it, the second I am keeping, and if you do not want to take the trouble of writing another letter, I am prepared to publish the letter that is before me. I am not aware of any offensive passage in it. But if I find any, you may depend upon my removing every such passage. I consider that letter to be a frank and honest document.

With love,

Bapu

CHAPTER 4

Nehru to Gandhi[1]

Allahabad,
23.1.1928

My dear Bapuji,

Your letter came as a bit of a shock and was painful reading. Painful because with relentless logic you had contemplated certain eventualities which I had not considered possible or even thought of in their entirety. You talk about my carrying on 'open warfare' against you and of 'unfurling my banner'. I have no particular banner to unfurl nor had I thought of the possibility of any warfare between you and me. I had certainly thought of differences of opinion, which may be fundamental, and of my following a line of action in regard to certain matters which may not meet with your approval. But I felt that you would certainly desire me to follow that line, even though you disagreed with it, if you thought that I was quite clear about it in my own mind. And even if there were possibilities of conflict on some points, there appeared to me absolutely no necessity for this differences or conflict to spread to the many other points on which I presumed there would be considerable ground for common action. You have referred to Shastri and your relations with him. Is any assurance from me necessary that nothing that can ever happen can alter or lessen my deep regard and affection for you? That regard and affection is certainly personal, but it is something more. No

[1] *Selected Works J.N.*, Vol. 3 (New Delhi, 1972), pp. 18–20.

one had moved me and inspired me more than you and I can never forget your exceeding kindness to me. There can be no question of our personal relations suffering. But even in the wider sphere am I not your child in politics, though perhaps a truant and errant child?

I should very much like to discuss many things with you and I cannot say whether I shall or shall not change many of my present opinions after my discussion with you. I hope I am not rigid in mind and outlook and nothing could please me more than to be convinced by you. I have wanted to have a good talk with you frequently in times past but you are always so busy and although I saw you often enough before I went to Europe I never had the opportunity I desired. I shall try to come to you as early as possible. Before I do so I shall write to you again and somewhat more fully some of the conclusions I have arrived at after some thought. I do not want to trouble you, specially in your present state of health, with long letters. But I think that if I write to you about my present views it would clarify matters and save time when we discuss them.

I do not quite appreciate your suggestion to publish my previous letter and to comment on it. Should you wish it of course you can do so. But it was an entirely personal letter and I do not see why the public should concern itself with it. Perhaps you may have been led to think that I am going to start some kind of a campaign against your ideas and it was desirable that before doing so some kind of statement should be issued. I have no such intention and if I criticize anything or defend anything against your wishes it will be done incidentally only. May I however warn you against believing everything that appears in the papers. The other day I spoke at Benares at a public meeting. I spoke in Hindi and my speech was wholly distorted in the English report and I was made to say something which I had never thought of. This was commented upon by the *Tribune* of Lahore, and may be other papers and it was made out that I was attacking you. This was a monstrous notion as I had not referred to you or thought of you in that connection. I have sent a contradiction. There is danger of this happening and I would beg of you not to believe such reports and to give me credit for greater sense and courtesy.

I would therefore suggest that for the present at least you might not publish my letter. But it is for you to judge and if you think it necessary you can publish extracts from it.

The last letter I received from father was not a cheerful document. He had evidently been upset by the doctor's reports about the state of his eyes and his heart. He has been told that if he does not take great care he may lose his sight. He talks in his letter of the 'approaching end' and appears to be very dispirited. I want to meet him in Bombay on February 6th when he lands. If he agrees I should like him to go with me to Sabarmati straight from Bombay.

Please do not trouble to answer this letter. There is nothing to answer. I shall try to follow it up after a week or so by another letter.

With love,

Yours affectionately,
Jawaharlal

CHAPTER 5

Gandhi to Nehru[1]

After 1 July 1929

My Dear Jawaharlal,

I read the current *Congress Bulletin.* I think that the reproduction of that statement [by Bhagat Singh and his comrades] was out of place in an official publication which is designed merely to record Congress activities. Is it not like a government gazette? On merits too I understand that it was prepared by their counsel. It is not the outpourings of earnest souls as you and I thought it was.

Nor did I like your advocacy and approval of the fast they are undergoing. In my opinion it is an irrelevant performance and in so far as it may be relevant it is like using Nasmyth hammer to crush a fly. However this is for you to ponder over.

I would like you to come to a decision soon regarding the Presidentship. Why this hesitation? I thought at Almora it was agreed that you would wear the crown. On this, read the enclosed and hand it on to Father.

I hope Kamala is well.

Yours,
Bapu

[1] *Collected Works M.G.*, Vol. XLI (New Delhi, 1970), pp. 152–3.

CHAPTER 6

Nehru to Gandhi[1]

Allahabad,
13.07.1929

My dear Bapuji,

I have your letter. About the presidentship, I wrote to you a few days ago and you must have got my letter soon after you wrote yours. My own personal inclination always is not to be shackled down to any office. I prefer to be free and to have time to act according to my own inclinations. But for years past I have been tied down to various offices and have had to give a great deal of my time to routine and other work to the exclusion of other matters to which I would have liked to attend to. On my return from Europe I had the fixed intention of spending a few months at least in some village areas, more or less cut off from outside activities. I wanted to try to organise them according to my own ideas but even more so I wanted to educate myself and try to get at the back of the mind of the villager. The Congress secretary duties and repeated and continuous calls for other work prevented me from doing this.

Somehow or other I cannot extricate myself from the tangle of activities I have got into. It seems even more difficult to extricate myself now than it has been. Now that it is proposed to take a really serious step in the near future, it is all the more difficult to think of retirement for a while to a village.

[1] *Selected Works J.N.*, Vol. 4 (New Delhi, 1973), pp. 156–7.

So far as I am concerned the presidentship will thus be a burden to me. Most others also are likely to consider it a burden and a nuisance. You will not of course be deceived by various odd persons here and there expressing their confidence in me. It is very good fortune that I have won the goodwill of a number of people but with this goodwill there is also a lack of confidence. I represent nobody but myself. I have not the politician's flair for forming groups and parties. My one attempt in this direction the formation of the Independence for India League last year was a hopeless failure so far as I was concerned. Instead of having a group of single-minded individuals cooperating together for a common object, I found that there was neither single mindedness nor cooperation and I was being compelled by force of circumstances to do things I was in thorough disagreement with.

Most people who put me forward for the presidentship do so because they want to keep someone else out. I am the lesser evil. This kind of negative backing is hardly good enough and does not enthuse.

If there is going to be effective action next year there can be no doubt that it will make all the differences in the world whether you lead it nor not. Of course you can lead, as you have done in the past, without being Congress President. But it would help matters certainly if you are also the official head of the organization. I feel that it would be a great gain if you would preside. That would strike the imagination of the country and other countries. If I have the misfortune to be President you will see that the very people who put me there, or many of them, will be prepared to cast me to the wolves.

Anyhow, I do not see why a final decision should be made now. The A.I.C.C. meeting this month is bound to have far-reaching results whichever way the decision goes. I think the best one can do is to wait till it is over.

I am sorry you disapproved of my giving Bhagat Singh and Dutt's statement in the *Congress Bulletin.* I was myself a little doubtful as to whether I should give it but when I found that there was very general appreciation of it among Congress circles I decided to give extracts. It was difficult however to pick and choose and gradually most of it went in. But I agree with you that it was somewhat out of place. I think you are mistaken in thinking that the statement was the work of their counsel. My information is that counsel had nothing, or practically nothing, to do with it. He might have touched up the punctuation.

I think the statement was undoubtedly a genuine thing.

Have I been advocating the fast? I had not intended doing so and I do not know to what statement of mine you are referring to. In Delhi I had stated that we could not help sympathizing with Bhagat Singh and Dutt during their long fast. As a matter of fact I am not in favour of hunger strikes. I told this to many young men who came to see me on this subject but I did not think it worthwhile to condemn the fast publicly.

Kamala had another attack three days ago but it was a short and mild one this time. My mother is now laid up with dengue fever.

Yours affectionately,
Jawaharlal

CHAPTER 7

Gandhi to Nehru[1]

2.5.1933

My Dear Jawaharlal,

As I was struggling against the coming fast, you were before me as it were in flesh and blood. But it was no use. How I wish I could feel that you had understood the absolute necessity of it. The Harijan movement is too big for mere intellectual effort. There is nothing so bad in all the world. And yet I cannot leave religion and therefore Hinduism. My life would be a burden to me, if Hinduism failed me. I love Christianity, Islam and many other faiths through Hinduism. Take it away and nothing remains for me. But I cannot tolerate it with untouchability—the high and low belief. Fortunately Hinduism contains a sovereign remedy for the evil. I have applied the remedy. I want you to feel, if you can, that it is well if I survive the fast and well also if the body dissolves in spite of the effort to live. What is it after all more perishable than a brittle chimney piece. You can preserve the latter intact for ten thousand years, but you may fail to keep the body intact even for a minute. And surely death is not an end to all effort. Rightly faced, it may be but the beginning of a nobler effort. But I won't convince you by argument, if you did not see the truth intuitively. I know that even if I do not carry your approval with me, I shall retain your precious love during all those days of ordeal.

[1] *Collected Works M.G.*, Vol. LV (New Delhi, 1973), p. 96.

I had your letter which I had thought I would answer at leisure. Well, God had willed otherwise. I had talks with Krishna. Of Sarup's work in Kathiawar I think I wrote to you. Kamala has not even sent me her address. There has been no letter from her for many days now. When you see her please give her and Indu my love. Kamala must not worry over the fast. If possible send me a wire.

Love from us all.

Bapu

CHAPTER 8

Nehru to Gandhi[1]

'Parnakuti', Poona
13.09.1933

My Dear Bapu,

In our recent conversation you will remember that I laid stress on the reiteration and clearer definition of our national objective. The objective of political independence has been finally laid down by the Congress and there is nothing to add to it or take away from it. We stand for complete Independence. Sometimes a little confusion arises because of vague phraseology and misleading propaganda and it is therefore as well to remove this confusion by a reiteration of our political demand. Even the word 'independence' is used with a variety of meanings. Obviously it must include, as the Congress has clearly and definitely laid down, full control of the army and of foreign relations as well as financial and economic control.

In regard to economic matters, the Karachi Congress by passing the important resolution on 'Fundamental Rights and Economic Policy' gave a lead and pointed out the direction in which we should move. I attach great importance to that resolution but I would personally like to go much further and to clarify the position still more.

It seems to me that if we are to improve the condition of the masses, to raise them economically and give them free-

[1] *Collected Works M.G.*, Vol. LV (New Delhi, 1973), pp. 457–60.

dom, it is inevitable that vested interests in India will have to give up their special position and many of their privileges. It is inconceivable to me how else the masses can rise. Therefore the problem of achieving freedom becomes one of revising vested interests in favour of the masses. To the extent this is done, to that extent only will freedom come. The biggest vested interest in India is that of the British Government; next come the Indian Princes; and others follow. We do not wish to injure any class or group and the divesting should be done as gently as possible and with every effort to avoid injury. But it is obvious that the divesting is bound to cause loss to the classes or groups which enjoy special privileges at the expense of the masses. It is also obvious that the process of divesting must be as speedy as possible to bring relief to the masses whose condition, as you know, is as bad as it can well be. Indeed economic forces themselves are acting with amazing rapidity today and breaking the old order. The big zamindari and taluqdari system in the United Provinces has largely collapsed, though it may be kept up for some time longer by outside agencies. Even the condition of the zamindars is very bad and the peasantry of course are in a far worse position.

We are all agreed that the Round Table Conference and its various productions are utterly useless to solve even one of India's many problems. As I conceive it, the Round Table Conference was an effort to consolidate the vested interests of India behind the British Government so as to face the rising and powerful national and economic movements in the country which threaten these interests. Essentially, in international parlance, it was a fascist grouping of vested and possessing interests, and fascist methods were adopted in India to suppress the national movement. And because the mere preservation of all these vested interests in India cannot possibly solve our economic ills, whether those of the masses or even of the middle classes, the effort is foredoomed to inevitable failure. Even from the point of view of a democratic nationalism, as you yourself stated at the Round Table Conference, democracy and autocracy can ill go together.

Another aspect has to be borne in mind. The problem of Indian freedom cannot be separated from the vital international problems of the world. The present crisis in world affairs is having its repercussions in India. At any moment it may result in a complete breakdown or in a violent international conflagration. Everywhere there is a conflict and a contest between the forces of progress and betterment of the masses and the forces of reaction and vested interests. We cannot remain silent witnesses to this titanic struggle for it affects us intimately. Both on the narrower ground of our own interests and the wider ground of International Welfare and human progress, we must, I feel, range ourselves with the progressive forces of the world. This ranging ourselves at present can of course be ideological only.

These are some of the larger issues that fill my mind and I am convinced, not only that we ignore them at our peril, but that a true appreciation of them will vitalize and give new meaning to our struggle for freedom which we must continue till the full objective is achieved.

These wider issues are of great importance but at present, as you know, the minds of large numbers of our countrymen are greatly exercised over immediate national problems and especially the question of carrying on the struggle. The statements that you and Sjt. M.S. Aney issued some time ago to guide the country have, I am afraid, produced some confusion and there has even been some resentment in regard to particular directions contained in them. There is a vague talk, in quarters which ought to know better, that the Congress has been dissolved. It is obvious that nothing of the kind has been done or could be done under the constitution. Your directions and those of Mr. Aney were, I take it, in the nature of advice or suggestions to meet a certain position that had arisen. The Congress continues as before but it is clear that it cannot function normally when Government declare its committees to be illegal.

There can be no regular offices or open activity. To recognize this fact and to adapt ourselves to it is not to wind up any Congress Committee, much less the Congress organization as a whole.

A necessary consequence from this was to avoid the possibility of a few newcomers who formed committees, when the old members and other reliable workers went to prison, or even individuals, committing the Congress to an undesirable course of action. As is known, we have had to face this risk in the past and unreliable persons have come to the helm of affairs in some local areas with the intention of obstructing and even stopping the very activities they were supposed to further. It thus becomes desirable to prevent such unreliable persons from exploiting the name of the Congress Committee. This of course does not prevent Congress workers in any area from cooperating together in an organized way for the furtherance of our programme.

Confusion has also arisen in the country about the implications of individual and mass civil disobedience. I appreciate to some extent the difference but this difference does not appear to me to be a fundamental one, as, in any event, civil disobedience is essentially an individual affair. Individual civil disobedience can develop into mass civil disobedience. Besides, you told me that if an organization felt strong enough to undertake the responsibility and the risk, it could, of its own initiative, take up mass civil disobedience. Indeed you were of opinion that a local organization could, in this manner go ahead in any direction which was not contrary to Congress methods or policy.

Stress was laid in your previous statement on the undesirability of secrecy, although you pointed out that there was nothing inherently illegitimate in secret methods. I think that most of us agree, and certainly I am of that opinion, that our movement is essentially an open one and secret methods do not fit in with it. Such methods, if indulged in to any large extent, are likely to change the whole character of the movement, as it has been conceived, and produce a certain amount of demoralization. Agreeing with this, some of us feel that, to some extent as for instance in communicating with each other or sending directions or keeping contacts, a measure of secrecy may be necessary. Perhaps secrecy is hardly the word for those activities and privacy would suit them better. Privacy of course is always open to all groups and individuals. Secrecy or the avoidance of it, as you said, cannot be made into a fetish.

But secrecy is certainly involved in the production of printed or duplicated news-sheets and bulletins. These bulletins have often served a useful purpose in the past in keeping contact between headquarters and districts and in sending information or directions. You pointed out to me the difficulties and undesirable consequences of running these secret presses and duplicating machines. Many good workers are tied up and have to avoid aggressive action; money has to be invested in such machines and frequently they are taken away by the police. Even from the practical point of view this continuous drain and tying up of workers is not desirable, and undoubtedly it sometimes results in demoralization. You suggested that the best way was to have handwritten copies of bulletins, etc., containing the name of the publisher. Generally, I agree with all this and appreciate the force of your argument. But I do feel that under certain circumstances it may be desirable for a local or provincial committee or group to issue bulletins of directions, etc., secretly. This must not be encouraged; indeed it should be discouraged, but a certain latitude in exceptional circumstances might be permitted.

There is one other small matter which seems to me rather ridiculous. It was right and proper, if I may say so, for you to court imprisonment by giving previous intimation of your intention to do so to the authorities. But is seems to me to be perfectly absurd for others, and even Congress volunteers, to send such notices or communications to the authorities. Any person desiring to offer civil resistance should openly carry on activities which further our cause and thus court arrest. He must not forget or ignore these activities and merely ask to be arrested.

This letter has become long enough. I do not mention here the many other matters which I had the privilege of discussing with you.

Yours affectionately,
Jawahar

CHAPTER 9

Gandhi to Nehru[1]

'Parnakuti', Poona
14.09.1933

My Dear Jawaharlal,

I am glad you have written so fully and frankly.

When, on my return from London at the end of 1931, I found you to have been suddenly snatched away from me,[2] I felt the separation keenly. I was, therefore, most anxious to meet you and exchange views.[3]

With much of what you have said in your letter I am in complete agreement. The experience gained after the Karachi Congress had, if possible, strengthened my faith in the main resolution and the economic programme referred to by you. I have no doubt in my mind that our goal can be no less than 'Complete Independence'. I am also in whole-hearted agreement with you when you say that without a material revision of vested interests the condition of the masses can never be improved. I believe, too, though I may not go as far as you do, that before India can become one homogeneous entity, the princes will have to part with much of their power and become popular representatives of the people over whom they

[1] *Collected Works M.G.*, Vol. LV (New Delhi, 1973), pp. 427–30.

[2] The addressee was arrested on 26 December 1931, while on his way to see Gandhiji, *vide* Vol. XLVIII.

[3] Gandhiji and Jawahrlal Nehru met and had long discussions from 10 September.

are ruling today. I can corroborate from first hand experience much of what you say about the Round Table Conference. Nor have I the slightest difficulty in agreeing with you that in these days of rapid intercommunication and a growing consciousness of the oneness of all mankind, we must recognize that our nationalism must not be inconsistent with progressive internationalism. India cannot stand in isolation and unaffected by what is going on in other parts of the world. I can, therefore, go the whole length with you and say that 'we should range ourselves with the progressive forces of the world'. But I know that though there is such an agreement between you and me in the enunciation of ideals, there are temperamental differences between us. Thus you have emphasized the necessity of a clear statement of the goal, but having once determined it, I have never attached importance to the repetition. The clearest possible definition of the goal and its appreciation would fail to take us there if we do not know and utilize the means of achieving it. I have, therefore, concerned myself principally with the conservation of the means and their progressive use. I know that if we can take care of them, attainment of the goal is assured. I feel too that our progress towards the goal will be in exact proportion to the purity of our means. If we can give an ocular demonstration of our uttermost truthfulness and non-violence, I am convinced that our statement of the national goal cannot long offend the interest which your letter would appear to attack. We know that the princes, the zamindars, and those who depend for their existence upon the exploitation of the masses, would cease to fear and distrust us, if we could but ensure the innocence of our methods. We do not seek to coerce any. We seek to convert them. This method may appear to be long, perhaps too long, but I am convinced that it is the shortest.

In the main I agree with your interpretation of Sjt. Aney's instructions and my note upon them. I am quite clear in my mind that had those instructions not been issued, the whole movement of civil resistance would have collapsed through growing internal weakness; for Congressmen were deluding themselves into the belief that there were organizations effectively functioning to which they could look for guidance, when, as a matter of fact, under the organized terrorism which the Ordinance Rule means, organized functioning of Congress Committees had become impossible. A false belief in the functioning of organizations, rendered illegal and largely impotent, was fast producing a demoralization which had to be arrested. There is no such thing as demoralization in civil resistance properly applied. You have said rightly that after all 'civil disobedience is essentially an individual affair'. I go a step further and say that so long as there is one civil resister offering resistance, the movement cannot die and must succeed in the end. Individual civil resisters do not need the aid of an organization. After all an organization is nothing without the individuals composing it. Sjt Aney's instructions were, therefore, I hold, an affective answer to the Ordinances and if only men and women belonging to the Congress will appreciate the necessity of those instructions with all their implications, the Ordinances will be rendered nugatory, at least so far as the resisters are concerned. They can form a nucleus around which an army of invincible civil resisters can be built up. Nothing in Sjt. Aney's instructions or in my note would warrant the supposition that they preclude organized action by Congressmen in any shape or form.

I would like to warn you against thinking that there is no fundamental difference between individual civil resistance and mass civil resistance. I think that the fundamental difference is implied in your own admission that 'it is essentially an individual affair'. The chief distinction between mass civil resistance and individual civil resistance is that in the latter everyone is a complete independent unit and his fall does not affect the others; in mass civil resistance the fall of one generally adversely affects the rest. Again, in mass civil resistance leadership is essential, in individual civil resistance every resister is his own leader. Then again, in mass civil resistance, there is a possibility of failure; in individual civil resistance failure is an impossibility. Finally, a State may cope with mass civil resistance; no State has yet been found able to cope with individual civil resistance.

Nor may much be made of my statement that an organization which feels its own strength can at its own risk adopt mass civil resistance. While, as an opinion, it is unexceptionable, I know that at the present moment there is no organization that can shoulder the burden. I do not want to raise false hopes.

Now about the secret methods. I am as firm as ever that they must be tabooed. I am myself unable to make any exceptions. Secrecy has caused much mischief and if it is not put down with a firm hand, it may ruin the movement. There may be exceptional circumstances that may warrant secret methods. I would forgo that advantage for the sake of the masses whom we want to educate in fearlessness. I will not confuse their minds by leading them to think that under certain circumstances, they may resort to secret methods. Secrecy is inimical to the growth of the spirit of civil resistance. If Congressmen will realize that all property is liable to be confiscated at any moment, they will learn to be utterly independent of it.

I quite agree with you that it is ludicrous for individuals to send notices to the local authorities of their intention to offer a particular form a civil disobedience. We do not want to make a great movement ridiculous. Therefore when civil resistance is offered it should be offered seriously and in an effective manner, in so far as this is possible, in furtherance of the Congress programme.

I notice one gap in your letter. You make no mention of the various constructive activities of the Congress. They became an integral part of the Congress programme that was framed after mature deliberations in 1920. With civil resistance as the background we cannot possibly do without the constructive activities such as communal unity, removal of untouchability and universalization of the spinning-wheel and *khaddar*. I am as strong as ever about these. We must recognize that whilst the Congressmen can be counted by hundreds of thousands civil resisters imprisoned have never amounted to more than one lakh at the outside. I feel that there is something radically wrong if paralysis has overtaken the remaining lakhs. There is nothing to be ashamed of in an open confession by those who for any reason whatsoever are unable to join the civil resister's ranks. They are also serving the cause of the country and bringing it nearer to the goal who are engaged in any of the constructive activities I have named and several other kindred activities I can add to the list. Ordinance or no Ordinance, if individual Congressmen and Congresswomen will learn the art of contributing their share to the work of building of the house of independence and realize their own importance, dark as the horizon seems to us, there is absolutely no cause for despair or disappointment.

Finally, if I can say so without incurring the risk of your accusing me of egotism, I would like to say that I have no sense of defeat in me and the hope in me that this country of ours is fast marching towards its goal is burning as bright as it did in 1920; for I have an undying faith in the efficacy of civil resistance. But as you are aware, after full and prayerful consideration, I have decided not to take the offensive during the unexpired period of the sentences of imprisonment that was pronounced against me on the 4th of August last by the court that met in Yeravada Jail. I need not go into the reasons as I have already issued a separate statement about it. This personal suspension, although it may be misunderstood for a while, will show how and when it may become a duty. And if it is duty, it cannot possibly injure the cause.

Yours,
Bapu

CHAPTER 10

Nehru to Gandhi[1]

Anand Bhawan,
Allahabad
13.08.1934

My dear Bapu,

After just six months of absolute seclusion and little exercise I have felt rather lost in the anxiety, excitement and activity of past 27 hours. I fell very tired. I am writing this letter to you at midnight. All day there have been crowds of people coming. If I have the chance I shall write to you again, but I doubt if I shall be able to do so for some months. I am, therefore, going to indicate to you briefly how I have reacted to the various major Congress decisions of the last five months or so. My sources of information have naturally been strictly limited but I think that they were sufficient to enable me to form a fairly correct idea of the general trend of events.

When I heard that you had called off the C.D. movement I felt unhappy. Only the brief announcement reached me at first. Much later I read your statement and this gave me one of the biggest shocks I have ever had. I was prepared to reconcile myself to the withdrawal C.D. But the reasons you gave for doing so and the suggestions you made for future work astounded me. I had a sudden and intense feeling that something broke inside me a bond that I had valued very

[1] *Collected Works M.G.*, Vol. LVIII (New Delhi, 1974), pp. 460–4 also *Selected Works J.N.*, Vol. 6 (New Delhi, 1974), pp. 277–82.

greatly had snapped. I felt terribly lonely in this wide world. I have always felt a little lonely almost from childhood up. But a few bonds strengthened me, a few strong supports held me up. That loneliness never went, but it was lessened. But now I felt absolutely alone, left high and dry on a desert island.

Human beings have an enormous capacity for adapting themselves and so I too adapted myself to some extent to the new conditions. The keenness of my feelings on the subject, which amounted almost to physical pain, passed off; the edge was dulled. But shock after shock, a succession of events sharpened that edge to a fine point, and allowed my mind or feelings no peace or rest. Again I felt that sensation of spiritual isolation, of being a perfect stranger out of harmony, not only with the crowds that passed me, but also with those whom I had valued as dear and close comrades. My stay in prison this time became a greater ordeal for my nerves than any previous visit had been. I almost wished that all newspapers might be kept away from me so that I might be spared these repeated shocks.

Physically I kept fairly well. I always do in prison. My body has served me well and can stand a great deal of ill-treatment and strain. And being vain enough to imagine that perhaps I might yet do some effective work in this land to which fate had tied me, I looked after it well.

But I wondered often enough if I was not a square peg in a round hole, or a bubble of conceit thrown about hither and thither on an ocean which spurned me. But vanity and conceit triumphed and the intellectual apparatus that functions within me refused to admit defeat. If the ideals that had spurred me to action and had kept me buoyed up through stormy weather were right—and the conviction of their rightness ever grew within me—they were bound to triumph though my generation might not live to witness that triumph.

But what had happened to those ideals during these long and weary months of this year when I was a silent and distant witness, fretting at my helplessness? Setbacks and temporary defeats are common enough in all great struggles. They grieve but one recovers soon enough. One recovers soon if the light of those ideals is not allowed to grow dim and the anchor of principles holds fast, But what I saw was not setback and defeat but that spiritual defeat which is the most terrible of all. Do not imagine that I am referring to the council-entry question. I do not attach vital importance to it. Under certain circumstances I can even imagine entering a legislature myself. But whether I function inside or outside the legislature I function as a revolutionary, meaning thereby a person working for the fundamental and revolutionary changes, political and social, for I am convinced that no other changes can bring peace or satisfaction to India and the world.

So I thought. Not so evidently the leaders who were functioning outside. They began to talk the language of an age gone by before the heady wine of N.C.O. and C.D. had fired our heads. Sometimes they used the same words and phrases but they were dead words without life or real meaning. The leading figures of the Congress suddenly became those people who had obstructed us, held us back, kept aloof from the struggle and even cooperated with the opposite party in the time of our direct need. They became the high priests in our temple of freedom and many a brave soldier who batch shouldered the burden in the heat and dust of the fray was not even allowed inside the temple precincts. He and many like him had become untouchables and unapproachable. And if he ventured to raise his voice and criticize the new high priests, he was shouted down and told that he was a traitor to the cause because he spoilt the harmony of the sacred precincts.

And so the flag of Indian freedom was entrusted with all pomp and circumstance to those who had actually hauled it down at the height of our national struggle at the bidding of the enemy; to those who had proclaimed from the house-tops that they had given up politics—for politics were unsafe then—but who emerged with a jump to the front ranks when politics became safe.

And what of the ideals they set forth before them, speaking as they did on behalf of the Congress and the nation? A pitiful hotchpotch, avoiding real issues, toning down, as far as they dared, even the political objective of the Congress, expressing a tender solicitude for every vested interest, bowing down to many a declared enemy of freedom, but showing great truculence and courage in facing the advanced and fighting elements in the Congress ranks. Is not the Congress being rapidly reduced to a magnified edition of that shameful spectacle, the Calcutta Corporation during the last few years? Might not the dominant part of the Bengal Congress be called today 'the society for the advancement of Mr. Nalini Ranjan Sirkar', a gentleman who rejoiced to entertain Government officials, Home Members and the like, when most of us were in prison and C.D. was supposed to be flourishing? And the other part probably a similar society by a similar laudable object? But the fault clouts not lie with Bengal alone. Almost everywhere there is a similar outlook. The Congress from top to bottom is a caucus and opportunism triumphs.

The Working Committee is not directly responsible for this state of affairs. But nonetheless the Working Committee must shoulder the responsibility. It is the leaders and their policy that shape the activities of the followers. It is neither fair nor just to throw blame on the followers. Every language has some saying about the workman blaming his tools. The committee had deliberately encouraged vagueness in the definition of our ideals and objectives and this is bound to lead not only to confusion but to demoralization during periods of reaction, and to the emergence of the demagogue and the reactionary.

I am referring especially to the political objectives which are the special province of the Congress. I feel that the time is overdue for the Congress to think clearly on social and economic issues but I recognize that education on these issues takes time and the Congress as a whole may not be able to go as far at present as I would like it to. But it appears that whether the Working Committee knows anything about the subject or not it is perfectly willing to denounce and to excommunicate people who happen to have made a special study of the subject and hold certain views. No attempt is manic to understand those views, which, it is notorious, are held by a very large number of the ablest and most self-sacrificing people in the world. Those views may be right or wrong but they deserve at least some understanding before the Working Committee sets out to denounce them. It is hardly becoming for a reasoned argument to be answered by sentimental appeals or by the cheap remark that the condition in India are different and the economic laws that apply elsewhere do not function here. The resolution of the Working Committee on the subject showed such an astounding ignorance of the elements of socialism that it was painful to read it and to realize that it might be read outside India. It seemed that the overmastering desire of the Committee was somehow to assure various vested interests even at the risk of talking nonsense.

A strange way of dealing with the subject of socialism is to use the word, which has a clearly defined meaning in the

English language, in a totally different sense. For individuals to use words in a sense peculiar to themselves is not helpful in the commerce of ideas. A person who declares himself to be an engine-driver and then adds that his engine is of wood and is drawn by bullocks is misusing the word engine-driver.

This letter has become a much longer one than I expected and the night is already far spent. Probably they have written in a confused and scrappy way for my brain is tired. But still it will convey some picture of my mind. The last few months have been very painful ones for me and, I take it, for many others. I have felt sometimes that in the modern world, and perhaps in the ancient world also, it is oft preferred to break some people's hearts rather than touch other's pockets. Pockets are indeed more valuable and more cherished than hearts and brains and bodies and human justice and dignity.

There is one other subject I should like to mention. That is the Swaraj Bhawan Trust. I understand that the Working Committee recently considered the question of the upkeep of the Swaraj Bhawan and came to the conclusion that it was not responsible for it. As however it had already made a grant about three years ago and this had not been paid yet, although expenses were incurred on the strength of it, a fresh grant was sanctioned. This will probably be enough for some months. In regard to the future, the Working Committee was evidently anxious not to be saddled with the burden of maintaining the house and grounds. This burden amounts to Rs.100 a month, which includes taxes, etc. The trustees, I understand, were also a little frightened of the burden and suggested that parts of the house might be let in the ordinary way to raise money for the maintenance. Another suggestion was made that part of the grounds might be sold off for this purpose. I was surprised to learn of these suggestions, as some of them seemed to me to be contrary to the letter of the trust and all of them against its spirit. As an individual trustee I have only one voice in the matter but I should like to say that I have the strongest possible objection to any such misuse of the trust property. The very idea of the wishes of my father being flouted in this way is intolerable to roe. The trust represented not only his wishes but also in a small way a memorial to him and his wishes and his memory is dearer to me than Rs. 100 a month. I should, therefore, like to assure the Working Committee and the trustees that they need have no anxiety on the score of the money required for maintenance of the property. As soon as the funds, now granted by the Working Committee for some months, are exhausted, I shall make myself personally responsible for the maintenance and no further grant need be made by the Working Committee. I would also beg the trustees to respect my feelings in this matter and not to break up the property or to hire it for the sake of hiring it out. I shall endeavour to maintain the Swaraj Bhawan property till such time as it is put to some worthy use.

I have not the figures by me but I believe that even thus far the Swaraj Bhawan has not been, in any sense, a financial burden on the Working Committee. The grants that have been paid to it will probably not be much in excess of reasonable rent for the quarters occupied by the office of the A.I.C.C. This rent could have been reduced by occupying smaller and cheaper quarters. At the same time in the past the A.I.C.C. has paid as much as Rs. 150 a month for rent of an upper floor only in Madras.

Perhaps some parts of this letter might pain you. But you would not have me hide my heart from you.

Yours affectionately,
Jawahar

CHAPTER 11

Gandhi to Nehru[1]

17.08.1934

My dear Jawaharlal,

Your passionate and touching letter deserves a much longer reply than my strength will permit.

I had expected fuller grace from the Government. However your presence has done for Kamala and incidentally for Mama what no drugs or doctors could have done. I hope that you will be allowed to remain longer than the very few days you expect.

I understand your deep sorrow. You are quite right in giving full and free expression to your feelings. But I am quite sure that from our common standpoint a closer study of the written word will show you that there is not enough reason for all the grief and disappointment you have felt. Let me assure you that you have not lost a comrade in me. I am the same as you knew me in 1917 and after. I have the same passion that you knew me to possess for the common goal. I want complete independence for the country in the full English sense of the term. And every resolution that has pained you had been framed with that end in view. I must take full responsibility for the resolutions and the whole conception surrounding them.

But I fancy that I have the knack for knowing the need of the time. And the resolutions are a response thereto. Of course

[1] *Collected Works M.G.*, Vol. LVIII (New Delhi, 1974), pp. 317–19.

here comes in the difference of our emphasis on the method or the means which to me are just as important as the goal and in a sense more important in that we have some control over them whereas we have none over the goal if we lose control over the means.

Do read the resolution about 'loose talk' dispassionately. There is not a word in it about socialism. Greatest consideration has been paid to the socialists some of whom I know so intimately. Do I not know their sacrifice? But I have found them as a body to be in a hurry. Why should they not be? Only, if I cannot march quite as quick, I must ask them to halt and take me along with them. That is literally my attitude. I have looked up the dictionary meaning of socialism. It takes me no further than where I was before I read the definition. What will you have me to read to know its full content? I have read one of the books Masani gave me and now I am devoting all my spare time to reading the book recommended by Narendra Deva.

You are hard on the members of the Working Committee. They are our colleagues such as they are. After all we are a free institution. They must be displaced, if they do not deserve confidence. But it is wrong to blame them for their inability to undergo the sufferings that some others have gone through.

After the explosion I want construction. Therefore now, lest we do not meet, tell me exactly what you will have me to do and who you think will best represent your views.

As to the trust, I was not present. Vallabhbhai was. Your attitude betrays anger. You should trust the trustees to do their duty. I did not think there was anything wrong. I was too preoccupied to concentrate on it. I shall now study the papers and everything. Of course your feelings will be fully respected by other trustees. Having given you this assurance,

I would ask you not to take this matter so personally as you have done. It more becomes your generous nature to give the same credit to your co-trustees for regard for Father's memory that you would take for yourself. Let the nation be custodian of Father's memory and you only as one of the nation.

I hope Indu is well and likes her new life. And what about Krishna?

Love.

Bapu

CHAPTER 12

Gandhi to Nehru[1]

03.10.1935

My Dear Jawaharlal,

Your letters come in with clock-like regularity and they are such a blessing.

I see that Kamala is putting forth a very brave effort. It will be rewarded. You know my partiality for nature-cure methods. There are in Germany itself many nature-cure establishments. Kamala's case may he past that stage. But one never knows. I know of cases which were reported to be for surgical treatment but which yielded to nature-cure treatment. I send you this experience of mine for what it is worth.

Your letter about the wearing of the next year's crown was delightful. I was glad to have your consent. I am sure that it would solve many difficulties and it is the rightest thing that could have happened for the country. Your presidentship at Lahore was totally different from what it would be at Lucknow. In my opinion it was comparatively plain sailing at Lahore in every respect. It won't be so in any respect at Lucknow. But those circumstances I cannot imagine anybody better able to cope with than you. May God give you all the strength to shoulder the burden.

I am going through your chapters[2] as speedily as I can. They are to me of absorbing interest. More than that I must not say just now.

This letter carries the love of us to you all.

Bapu

[1] *Collected Works M.G.*, Vol. LXII (New Delhi, 1975), p. 6.

[2] Of Nehru's *Autobiography.*

CHAPTER 13

Nehru to Gandhi[1]

Allahabad
5.7.1936

My Dear Bapu,

I arrived here last night. Ever since I left Wardha[2] I have been feeling weak in body and troubled in mind. Partly this is no doubt due to physical causes—a chill which has aggravated my throat trouble. But partly also it is due to other causes which touch the mind and the spirit directly. Since my return from Europe, I have found that meetings of the Working Committee exhaust me greatly; they have a devitalizing effect on me and I have almost the feeling of being older in years after every fresh experience. I should not be surprised if this feeling was also experienced by my colleagues of the Committee. It is an unhealthy experience and it comes in the way of effective work.

I was told, when I returned from Europe, that the country was demoralized and hence we had to go slow. My own little experience during the past four months has not confirmed this impression. Indeed I have found a bubbling vitality wherever I have gone and I have been surprised at the public response. What this is due to I cannot say definitely. I can only make various guesses. This public response has naturally

[1] *Selected Works J.N.*, Vol. 7 (New Delhi, 1975), pp. 309–13.

[2] Jawaharlal had gone to Wardha to attend the Working Committee meeting held from 29 June to 1 July 1936.

heartened me and filled me with fresh energy. But this energy seems to ooze out of me at every meeting of the Working Committee and I return feeling very much like a discharged battery. The reaction has been greatest on this occasion because of my being physically in a low condition.

But it was not about my physical or mental condition that I wished to write to you. There are more important matters which worry me and so far I have seen no clear way out. I do not wish to act in a hurry or without giving the fullest thought to the matter. But even before my own mind is decided I want to tell you which way I am looking.

I am grateful to you for all the trouble you took in smoothing over matters and in-helping to avoid a crisis. I was convinced then and I am convinced now that a break of the kind suggested would have had serious consequences for all our work, including the elections. And yet, where are we now and what does the future hold for us? I read again Rajendra Babu's letter to me (the second one) and his formidable indictment of me. That indictment, though formidable, is not specific, except for my speech at the women's meeting, which, as a matter of fact, has nothing to do with any wider issue. The main thing is that my activities are harmful to the Congress cause. They are doing damage to the Congress and are lessening its chances of success at the elections. If I continue in this way there is likely to be further deterioration and my colleagues do not wish to take any chances in this vital matter.

Now, obviously, if there is any truth in this charge it must be faced. The matter is too serious to be glossed over. There are no black and white shades, no delicate balancing of the resultant good or evil; it is all black and that really makes it easier to decide. For however tenderly the fact may be stated, it amounts to this: that I am an intolerable nuisance and the very qualities I possess—a measure of ability, energy, earnestness, some personality which has a vague appeal—become dangerous for they are harnessed to a wrong chariot. The conclusion from all this is obvious.

My own impression before Lucknow, and to some extent even at Lucknow, was that it should not be difficult for all of us to pull together this year. It is evident now that I was mistaken, though there has been no lack of trying on either side. Perhaps the fault may lie with me; I am not aware of it; but one can seldom see the beam in one's own eye. The fact remains, and today there is no loyalty of the spirit which binds our group together. It is a mechanical group and on either side there is a dull resentment and a sense of suppression, and that, as every student of psychology knows, results in all manner of undesirable complexes, both individual and social.

When I reached Bombay this time many people stared hard at me finding it difficult to believe how I had survived. It seemed to be common knowledge there (as reported in *The Times of India* previously) that a peaceful end awaited me—politically, of course. All had been fixed up except the cremation. Hence the surprise. It struck me as curious that I should be wholly ignorant of all these confident rumours when many people in the street were full of them. But though I had been ignorant of them, the rumours had the strongest justification. That in itself is a measure of my present isolation.

I have written at length, both in my book and subsequently, about my present ideas. There is no lack of material for me to be judged. Those views are not casual. They are part of me and, though I might change them or vary them in future, so long as I hold them I must give expression to them. Because I attached importance to a larger unity I tried to express them in the mildest way possible and more as an invitation to thought than as fixed conclusions. I saw no conflict in this approach and in anything that the Congress was doing. So far as the elections were concerned I felt definitely that my approach was a definite asset to us as it enthused the masses. But my approach, mild and vague as it was, is considered dangerous and harmful by my colleagues. I was even told that my laying stress always on the poverty and unemployment in India was unwise, or at any rate the way I did it was wrong.

You will remember that both in Delhi and in Lucknow I made it clear that I must have freedom to express my views on social matters. I understood you and the members of the Committee to agree to this. The question now becomes one more of this freedom of expression than of the views themselves. Even more so it is a question of values in life, and if we value anything greatly we may not sacrifice it.

There is this undeniable conflict. Who is right and who is wrong it is futile to argue. But after last week's incidents I am beginning to doubt if we are really following the correct course. I am inclined to think that the right thing for us to do will be to put the matter briefly before the A.I.C.C. at its next meeting and take its direction in the matter. How best to do this I am not clear yet but it should be done as simply as possible and without much argument. So far as I am concerned there will be little argument.

Presumably the result of this will be that I shall retire and a more homogeneous Committee will be formed.

You told me that you intended issuing some kind of a statement. I shall welcome this for I believe in every viewpoint being placed clearly before the country.

I am not mentioning this matter to anyone yet. Of course prying and impertinent eyes will see this *en route* even before it reaches you. They have to be suffered.

In Bombay I had a talk with Mridula. She came from Ahmedabad for a few hours especially at my request. She gave me to understand that, so far as facts were concerned, she had noticed (or mentioned) no difference between what you had told her and what I had written or said. She had indeed made this clear in her letter to you but perhaps you missed a sentence or two. She proposed to send you a copy of her previous letter so that you might see this for yourself.

I was told in Wardha that it was being said by Gujarat women that you or Vallabhbhai or both were responsible for the exclusion of women from the Working Committee. I enquired from Mridula. She told me that to her knowledge nobody had said so or thought so.

I also had a talk with Sarojini on this subject.

I met Jivraj Mehta and Khurshed. Jivraj did not quite agree with Bidhan about the cost, etc. But he brought down his previous figure somewhat. He now says that two lakhs ought to be enough for the construction, equipment, etc., of the hospital. He would like to see another two lakhs as a reserve fund. He is also of opinion that the construction should be made not on the Swaraj Bhawan grounds, as originally planned, but on the fields to the east of Anand Bhawan. I shall make enquiries from the municipality about this.

I propose to convene a meeting of the Kamala Memorial trustees in Bombay about the time the A.I.C.C. meets. Also a meeting of the Swaraj Bhawan trustees.

In Bombay Nargis insisted on sending me to a German that specialist and this man has told me to remain almost absolutely silent for a week in order to rest my throat. It is a hard job.

Yours affectionately,
Jawaharlal

CHAPTER 14

Gandhi to Nehru[1]

Segaon, Wardha
8.7.1936

My Dear Jawaharlal,

I have just received your letter. I was seeking time to be able to write to you on the events in Wardha. Your letter makes it difficult. I would however just like to say that the letter of withdrawal does not bear the meaning you put upon it when it was given to you. It was sent to you after I had seen it. The sending of such a letter in the place of resignation was my suggestion. I wish that you could take a juster view of that letter. In any case I am firmly of opinion that during the remainder of the year, all wrangling should cease and no resignations should take place. A.I.C.C. will be paralysed and powerless to deal with the crisis. It will be torn between two emotions. It would be most unfair to spring upon a crisis, in the name of democracy, which it has never been called upon it to face. You are exaggerating the implications of the letter. I must not argue. But I would urge you to consider the situation calmly and not succumb to it in a moment of depression so unworthy of you. Why should you not allow your humour to play upon the meetings of the W.C.? Why should it be so difficult for you to get on with those with whom you have worked without a jar for years? If they are guilty of intolerance,

[1] *Collected Works M.G.*, Vol. LXIII (New Delhi, 1976), pp. 127–8.

you have more than your share of it. The country should not be made to suffer for your mutual intolerance.

I do hope you have accepted the very sane advice of the German doctor.

Love.

Bapu

CHAPTER 15

Gandhi to Nehru[1]

Segaon, Wardha
15.7.1936

Dear Jawaharlal,

. . . . . .

Your letter is touching. You feel to be the most injured party. The fact is that your colleagues have lacked your courage and frankness. The result has been disastrous. I have always pleaded with them to speak out to you freely and fearlessly. But having lacked the courage, whenever they have spoken they have done it clumsily and you have felt irritated. I tell you they have dreaded you, because of your irritability and impatience of them. They have chafed under your rebukes and magisterial manner and above all your arrogation of what has appeared to them your infallibility and superior knowledge. They feel that you have treated them with scant courtesy and never defended them from socialists' ridicule and even misrepresentation.

You complain of their having called your activities harmful. That was not to say that you were harmful. Their letter was no occasion for recounting your virtues or your services. They were fully conscious of your dynamism and your hold over the masses and the youth of the country. They know that you cannot be dispensed with. And so they wanted to give way.

I look upon the whole affair as a tragic-comedy. I would

[1] *Collected Works M.G.*, Vol. LXIII (New Delhi, 1976), pp. 144–5.

therefore like you to look at the whole thing in a lighter vein. I do not mind your taking the A.I.C.C. into your confidence. But I do want you not to impose on it the unbearable task of adjusting your family quarrels or choosing between them and you. Whatever you do you must face them with accomplished things.

Why do you resent their majority being reflected in all subcommittees, etc.? Is it not the most natural thing? You are in office by their unanimous choice but you are not in power yet. To put you in office was an attempt to find you in power, quicker than you would otherwise have been. Anyway that was at the back of my mind when I suggested your name for the crown of thorns. Keep it on though the head be bruised. Resume your humour at the committee meetings. That is your most usual role not that of a care-worn irritable man ready to burst on the slightest occasion.

How I wish you could telegraph to me that on finishing my letter you felt as merry as you were on that New Year's Day in Lahore when you were reported to have danced round the tricolour flag.

You must give your throat a chance.

I am revising my statement. I have decided not to publish it till you have seen it.

I have decided that nobody should see our correspondence, besides Mahadev.

Love.

Bapu

CHAPTER 16

Gandhi to Nehru[1]

5.10.1945

Chi. Jawaharlal,

I have long been intending to write to you but can do so only today. I have also been wondering whether I should write in English or Hindustani. In the end I have decided to write in Hindustani.

I take first the sharp difference of opinion that has arisen between us. If such a difference really exists people should also know about it, for the work of swaraj will suffer if they are kept in the dark. I have said that I fully stand by the kind of governance which I have described in *Hind Swaraj*. It is not just a way of speaking. My experience has confirmed the truth of what I wrote in 1909. If I were the only one left who believed in it, I would not be sorry. For I can only testify to the truth as I see it. I have not *Hind Swaraj* in front of me. It is better that I redraw the picture today in my own Language. Then it would not matter to me whether or no the picture tallies with that of 1909, nor should it to you. I do not have to establish what I had said before. What is worth knowing is only what I have to say today. I believe that if India, and through India the world, is to achieve real freedom, then sooner or later we shall have to go and live in the villages—in huts, not in palaces. Millions of people can never live in cities and palaces in comfort and peace. Nor can they do so by

[1] *Collected Works M.G.*, Vol. LXXXI (New Delhi, 1980), pp. 319–21.

killing one another, that is, by resorting to violence and untruth. I have not the slightest doubt that, but for the pair, truth and non-violence, mankind will be doomed. We can have the vision of that truth and non-violence only in the simplicity of the villages. That simplicity resides in the spinning-wheel and what is implied by the spinning-wheel. It does not frighten me at all that the world seems to be going in the opposite direction. For the matter of that, when the moth approaches its doom it whirls round faster and faster till it is burnt up. It is possible that India will not be able to escape this moth-like circling. It is my duty to try, till my last breath, to save India and through it the world from such a fate. The sum and substance of what I want to say is that the individual person should have control over the things that are necessary for the sustenance of life. If he cannot have such control the individual cannot survive. Ultimately, the world is made up only of individuals. If there were no drops there would be no ocean. This is only a rough and ready statement. There is nothing new in this.

But even in *Hind Swaraj* I have not said all this. While I appreciate modern thought, I find that an ancient thing, considered in the light of this thought looks so sweet. You will not be able to understand me if you think that I am talking about the villages of today. My ideal village still exists only in my imagination. After all every human being lives in the world of his own imagination. In this village of my dreams the villager will not be dull—he will be all awareness. He will not live like an animal in filth and darkness. Men and women will live in freedom, prepared to face the whole world. There will be no plague, no cholera and no smallpox. Nobody will be allowed to be idle or to wallow in luxury. Everyone will have to do body labour. Granting all this, I can still envisage a number of things that will have to be organized on a large scale. Perhaps there will even be railways and also post and telegraph offices. I do not know what things there will be or will not be. Nor am I bothered about it. If I can make sure of the essential thing, other things will follow in due course. But if I give up the essential thing, I give up everything.

The other day, at the final day's meeting of the Working Committee, we had taken a decision to the effect that the Working Committee would meet for two or three days to work out this very thing. I shall be happy if it meets. But even if it does not meet, I want that we two should understand each other fully. And this for two reasons. Our bond is not merely political. It is much deeper. I have no measure to fathom that depth. This bond can never be broken. I therefore want that we should understand each other thoroughly in politics as well. The second reason is that neither of us considers himself as worthless. We both live only for India's freedom, and will be happy to die too for that freedom. We do not care for praise from any quarter. Praise or abuses are the same to us. They have no place in the mission of service. Though I aspire to live up to 125 years rendering service, I am nevertheless an old man, while you are comparatively young. That is why I have said that you are my heir. It is only proper that I should at least understand my heir and my heir in turn should understand me. I shall then be at peace. One thing more. I had written to you about Kasturba Trust and Hindustani. You had said you would write after thinking things over. I find that your name is already figuring in the Hindustani Sabha. Nanavati reminded me that he had approached you and Maulana Saheb and that you had appended your signature. That was in 1942. That was long ago. You know where Hindustani stands today. If you still stand by that signature, I wish to get some work out of you in this regard. It will not involve much running about, but some work will be called for. The work of Kasturba Memorial Trust is rather complicated. I realize that if what I have said above is going to irk you or is irking you, you will not feel comfortable even in the Kasturba Trust.

....

You are working very hard. I trust you are in good health and Indu is well.

Blessings from
Bapu

CHAPTER 17

Nehru to Gandhi[1]

Allahabad
9.10.1945

My dear Bapu,

I have received today, on return from Lucknow, your letter of the 5th October[2]. I am glad you have written to me fully and I shall try to reply at some length but I hope you will forgive me if there is some delay in this, as I am at present tied up with close-fitting engagements. I am only here now for a day and a half. It is really better to have informal talks but just at present I do not know when to fit this in. I shall try.

Briefly put my view is that the question before us is not one of truth *versus* untruth or non-violence *versus* violence. One assumes as one must that true cooperation and peaceful methods must be aimed at and a society which encourages these must be our objective. The whole question is how to achieve this society and what its content should be. I do not understand why a village should necessarily embody truth and non-violence. A village, normally speaking, is backward intellectually and culturally and no progress can be made from a backward environment. Narrow-minded people are much more likely to be untruthful and violent.

[1] *Selected Works J.N.*, Vol. 14 (New Delhi, 1981), pp. 554–7. There are printing errors in this volume, Gandhi's letter is mentioned as dated 2 October 1945 instead of 5 October 1945 and Nehru's letter dated 4 October 1945 instead of 9 October 1945.

[2] *Collected Works M.G.*, Vol. LXXXI (New Delhi, 1980), pp. 319–21. See the chapter no. 16 in this book.

Then again we have to put down certain objectives like a sufficiency of food, clothing, housing, education, sanitation, etc., which should be the minimum requirement for the country and for everyone. It is with these objectives in view that we must find out specifically how to attain them speedily. Again it seems to me inevitable that modern means of transport as well as many other modern developments must continue and be developed. There is no way out of it except to have them. If that is so inevitably a measure of heavy industry exists. How far will that fit in with a purely village society? Personally I hope that heavy or light industries should all be decentralized as far, as possible and this is feasible now because of the development of electric power. If two types of economy exist in the country either there should be conflict between the two or one will overwhelm the other.

The question of independence and protection from foreign aggression, both political and economic, has also to be considered in this context. I do not think it is possible for India to be really independent unless she is a technically advanced country. I am not thinking for the moment in terms of just armies but rather of scientific growth. In the present context of the world we cannot even advance culturally without a strong background of scientific research in every department. There is today in the world a tremendous acquisitive tendency both in individuals and groups and nations, which leads to conflicts and wars. Our entire society is based on this more or less. That basis must go and be transformed into one of cooperation, not of isolation which is impossible. If this is admitted and is found feasible then attempts should be made to realize it not in terms of an economy which is cut off from the rest of the world but rather one which cooperates. From the economic or political point of view an isolated India may well be a kind of vacuum which increases the acquisitive tendencies of others and thus creates conflicts.

There is no question of palaces for millions of people. But there seems to be no reasons why millions should not have comfortable up to date homes where they can lead a cultured existence. Many of the present overgrown cities have developed evils which are deplorable. Probably we have to discourage this overgrowth and at the same time encourage the village to approximate more to the culture of the town.

It is many years ago since I read *Hind Swaraj* and I have only a vague picture in my mind. But even when I read it 20 or more years ago it seemed to me completely unreal. In your writings and speeches since then I have found much that seemed to me an advance on that old position and an appreciation of modern trends. I was therefore surprised when you told us that the old picture still remains intact in your mind. As you know, the Congress has never considered that picture, much less adopted it. You yourself have never asked it to adopt it except for certain relatively minor aspects of it. How far it is desirable for the Congress to consider these fundamental questions, involving varying philosophies of life, it is for you to judge. I would imagine that a body like the Congress should not lose itself in arguments over such matters which can only produce great confusion in people's minds resulting in inability to act in the present. This may also result in creating barriers between the Congress and others in the country. Ultimately of course this and other questions will have to be decided by representatives of free India. I have a feeling that most of these questions are thought of and discussed in terms of long ago, ignoring the vast changes that have taken place all over the world during the last generation or more. It is 38 years since *Hind Swaraj* was written. The world has completely changed since then, possibly in a wrong direction. In any event any consideration of these questions must keep present facts, forces and the human material we have today in view, otherwise it will be divorced from reality. You are right in saying that the world, or a large part of it, appears to be bent on committing suicide. That may be an inevitable development of an evil seed in civilization that has grown. I think it is so. How to get rid of this evil, and yet how to keep the good in the present as in the past is our problem. Obviously there is good, too, in the present.

These are some random thoughts hurriedly written down and I fear they do injustice to the grave import of the questions raised, You will forgive me, I hope, for this jumbled presentation. Later I shall try to write more clearly on the subject.

....

I hope you are keeping well and have completely recovered from the attack of influenza.

Yours affectionately,
Jawahar

CHAPTER 18

Gandhi to Nehru[1]

Poona,
13.11.1945

Chi. Jawaharlal,

I was very happy with our talks yesterday. We could not have discussed more yesterday and it is my view that we shall not be able to finish our work at a single sitting. We must meet from time to time. I am so made that if I had the strength to travel about, I would seek you out, stay with you for a day or two, have some talk and then leave. Though I am not in a position to do that now, you may know I have done such things before. I want that people should know us as we know each other. If in the end we find that our paths are different, then so be it. Our hearts will still remain one, for they are one. The talks we had yesterday have given me the impression that there is not much difference in our outlooks or the way we understand things. I want to tell you how I have understood you. If there is any difference you will let me know.

(1) The crucial question according to you, is how to ensure man's mental, economic, political and moral development. That is my position too.
(2) And in doing so every individual should have equal right and opportunity.

[1] *Collected Works M.G.*, Vol. LXXXII (New Delhi, 1980), pp. 71–2.

(3) From this point of view there should be equality between villages and cities. And therefore their food and drink, their way of life, their dress and their habits should be the same. If such a condition is to be brought about people should produce their own cloth and food and build their own houses. So also they should produce their own water and electricity.

(4) Man is not born to live in the jungle; he is born to live in society. If we are to make sure that one person does not ride on another's back, the unit should be an ideal village or a social group which will be self-sufficient, but the members of which will be interdependent. This conception will bring about a change in human relationship all over the world.

If I have understood you correctly up to here, I shall take up the second part. I have had Rajkumari translate the letter which I wrote to you earlier. I am getting this also translated and will send the translation along with this. I serve two purposes by getting the letters translated. First I can explain to you more clearly in English what I want to say and secondly I shall be able to know better whether I have understood you fully or not.

Blessings to Indu.

Blessings from
Bapu

CHAPTER 19

Gandhi to Nehru[1]

18.01.1948

Chi. Jawaharlal,

Give up your fast....

May you live long and continue to be the jewel of India.

Blessings from
Bapu

[1] *Collected Works M.G.*, Vol. XC (New Delhi, 1994), p. 449.

After breaking his fast, when Gandhiji came to know that Jawaharlal Nehru was also fasting, he promptly wrote the letter in his own hand in spite of his extreme weakness.

CHAPTER 20

Nehru's Note to Dorothy Norman[1]

Below is an English translation of a letter which Gandhiji sent me. The original is in Hindi. It was written on the day he broke his fast which had already lasted a number of days and which was undertaken to indicate his unhappiness at the communal tension in Delhi.

I was rather upset at events in Delhi as well as Gandhiji's fast and for a day or two I did not take any food. This was not a regular fast but rather personal reaction to events which hardly anyone knew. Somehow, Gandhiji got to know of it and hence his advice to me to put an end to it.

The reference to a 'jewel of India' is a pun on my name Jawahar which means jewel.

This was the last letter [Gandhiji] wrote to me. Twelve days later, on 30 January 1948, he died at the hands of an assassin.

'My dear Jawaharlal,

Give up your fast.... May you live long and continue to be the jewel of India!

Blessings from
Bapu'

[1] *Sellected Works J.N.*, Vol. 5, second series (New Delhi, 1987), p. 585. Nehru wrote this note to Dorothy Norman, an American journalist and friend of the Nehru family, when she was collecting material for her book, *Nehru: The First Sixty Years,* published in New York in 1965.

PART TWO
APPENDICES

APPENDIX 1

Resolution on Fundamental Rights and Duties and Economic and Social Programme as Adopted by the Karachi Congress (March 1931) and Finalized by the Bombay AICC (August 1931)[1]

This Congress is of opinion that to enable the masses to appreciate what 'Swaraj', as conceived by the Congress, will mean to them, it is desirable to state the position of the Congress in a manner easily understood by them. In order to end the exploitation of the masses, political freedom must include real economic freedom of the starving millions. The Congress, therefore, declares that any Constitution which may be agreed to on its behalf should provide, or enable the Swaraj Government to provide, for the following:

(1) Every citizen of India has the right of free expression of opinion, the rights of free association and combination, and the right to assemble peacefully and without arms, for purposes not opposed to law or morality.

(2) Every citizen shall enjoy freedom of conscience and the right freely to profess and practice his religion, subject to public order and morality.

(3) The culture, language and script of the minorities and of the different linguistic areas shall be protected.

(4) All citizens are equal before the law, irrespective of caste, creed or sex.

(5) No disability attaches to any citizen, by reason of his or her religion, caste, creed or sex, in regard to public employment, office of power or honour, and in the exercise of any trade or calling.

[1] *Collected Works M.G.*, Vol. XLVII (New Delhi, 1971), pp. 260–5.

(6) All citizens have equal rights and duties in regard to wells, tanks, roads, schools and places of public resort, maintained out of State or local funds, or dedicated by private persons for the use of the general public.

(7) Every citizen has the right to keep and bear arms, in accordance with regulations and reservations made in that behalf.

(8) No person shall be deprived of his liberty nor shall his dwelling or property be entered, sequestered or confiscated, save in accordance with law.

(9) The State shall observe neutrality in regard to all religions.

(10) The franchise shall be on the basis of universal adult suffrage.

(11) The State shall provide for free and compulsory primary education.

(12) The State shall confer no titles.

(13) There shall be no capital punishment.

(14) Every citizen is free to move throughout India and to stay and settle in any part thereof, to acquire property and to follow any trade or calling, and to be treated equally with regard to legal prosecution or protection in all parts of India.

2.(a) The organization of economic life must conform to the principle of justice, to the end that it may secure a decent standard of living.

(b) The State shall safeguard the interests of industrial workers and shall secure for them, by suitable legislate and in other ways, a living wage, healthy conditions of work, limited hours of labour, suitable machinery for the settlement of disputes between employers and workmen, and protection against the economic consequences of old age, sickness and unemployment.

3. Labour to be freed from serfdom and conditions bordering on serfdom.
4. Protection of women workers, and specially, adequate provision for leave during maternity period.
5. Children of school going age shall not be employed in mines and factories.
6. Peasants and workers shall have the right to form unions to protect their interests.
7. The system of land tenure and revenue and rent shall be reformed and an equitable adjustment made of the burden on agricultural land, immediately giving relief to the small peasantry by a substantial reduction of agricultural rent and revenue now paid by them and in case of uneconomic holdings, exempting them from rent, so long as necessary, with such relief as may be just and necessary, to holders of small estates affected by such exemption or reduction in rent, and to the same end, imposing a graded tax on net income from land above a reasonable minimum.
8. Death duties on a graduated scale shall be levied on property above a fixed minimum.
9. There shall be a drastic reduction of Military expenditure so as to bring it down to at least one-half of the present scale.
10. Expenditure and salaries in civil departments shall be largely reduced. No servant of the State, other than specially employed experts and the like, shall be paid above a certain fixed figure, which should not ordinarily exceed Rs.500 per month.
11. No duty shall be levied on salt manufactured in India.
12. The State shall protect indigenous cloth; and for this purpose pursue the policy of exclusion of foreign cloth and foreign yarn from the country and adopt such other

measures as may be found necessary. The State shall also protect other indigenous industries, when necessary, against foreign competition.

13. Intoxicating drinks and drugs shall be totally prohibited, except for medicinal purposes.
14. Currency and exchange shall be regulated in the national interest.
15. The State shall own or control key industries and services, mineral resources, railways, waterways, shipping and other means of public transport.
16. Relief of agricultural indebtedness, and control of usury—direct and indirect.
17. The State shall provide for the Military training of citizens so as to organize a means of national defence apart from the regular Military forces.

APPENDIX 2

Congress Working Committee's Statement on India and the War Crisis,[1] *14 September 1939*

The Working Committee have given their earnest consideration to the grave crisis that has developed owing to the declaration of war in Europe. The principles which should guide the nation in the event of war have been repeatedly laid down by the Congress, and only a month ago this Committee reiterated them and expressed their displeasure at the flouting of Indian opinion by the British Government in India. As a first step to dissociate themselves from this policy of the British Government, the Committee called upon the Congress members of the Central Legislative Assembly to refrain from attending the next session. Since then the British Government have declared India as a belligerent country, promulgated Ordinances, passed the Government of India Act Amending Bill, and taken other far-reaching measures which affect the Indian people vitally, and circumscribe and limit the powers and activities of the provincial governments. This has been done without the consent of the Indian people whose declared wishes in such matters have been deliberately ignored by the British Government. The Working Committee must take the gravest view of these developments.

The Congress has repeatedly declared its entire disapproval of the ideology and practice of Fascism and Nazism and their glorification of war and violence and the suppression of the human spirit. It has condemned the aggressions in which they have repeatedly indulged and their sweeping away

[1] Bimal Prasad, *The Origins of Indian Foreign Policy: The Indian National Congress and World Affairs, 1885–1947* (Calcutta, 1963), pp. 308–15.

of well-established principles and recognized standards of civilized behaviour. It has seen in Fascism and Nazism the intensification of the principle of Imperialism against which the Indian people have struggled for many years. The Working Committee must, therefore, unhesitatingly condemn the latest aggression of the Nazi Government in Germany against Poland and sympathize with those who resist it.

The Congress has further laid down that the issue of war and peace for India must be decided by the Indian people, and no outside authority can impose this decision upon them, nor can the Indian people permit their resources to be exploited for Imperialist ends. Any imposed decision, or attempt to use India's resources for purposes not approved by them will necessarily have to be opposed by them. If cooperation is desired in a worthy cause, this cannot be obtained by compulsion and imposition, and the Committee cannot agree to the carrying out by the Indian people of orders issued by external authority. Cooperation must be between equals by mutual consent for a cause which both consider to be worthy. The people of India have, in the recent past, faced great risks and willingly made great sacrifices to secure their own freedom and establish a free democratic state in India, and their sympathy is entirely on the side of democracy and freedom. But India cannot associate herself in a war said to be for democratic freedom when that very freedom is denied to her and such limited freedom as she possesses taken away from her.

The Committee are aware that the Governments of Great Britain and France have declared that they are fighting for democracy and freedom and to put an end to aggression. But the history of the recent past is full of examples showing the constant divergence between the spoken word, the ideals proclaimed, and the real motives and objectives. During the war of 1914–18, the declared war aims were preservation of democracy, self-determination, and the freedom of small nations, and yet the very Governments which solemnly proclaimed these aims entered into secret treaties embodying imperialist designs for the carving up of the Ottoman Empire. While stating that they did not want any acquisition of territory, the victorious powers added largely to their colonial domains. The present European war itself signifies that abject failure of the Treaty of Versailles and of its makers, who broke their pledged word and imposed an imperialist peace on the defeated nations. The one hopeful outcome of that Treaty, the League of Nations, was muzzled and strangled at the outset and later killed by its parent states.

Subsequent history has demonstrated afresh how even a seemingly fervent declaration of faith may be followed by an ignoble desertion. In Manchuria the British Government connived at aggression; in Abyssinia they acquiesced in it. In Czechoslovakia and Spain democracy was in peril and it was deliberately betrayed, and the whole system of collective security was sabotaged by the very powers who had previously declared their firm faith in it.

Again it is asserted that democracy is in danger and must be defended and with this statement the Committee are in entire agreement. The Committee believe that the peoples of the West are moved by this ideal and objective and for these they are prepared to make sacrifices. But again and again the ideals and sentiments of people and of those who have sacrificed themselves in the struggle have been ignored and faith has not been kept with them.

If the war is to defend the *status quo*, imperialist possession, colonies, vested interests and privilege, then India can have nothing to do with it. If, however, the issue is democracy and a world order based on democracy, then India is intensely interested in it. The Committee are convinced that the interests of Indian democracy do not conflict with the interests of British democracy or of world democracy. But there is an inherent and ineradicable conflict between democracy for India or elsewhere and Imperialism and Fascism. If Great Britain fights for the maintenance and extension of democracy, then she must necessarily end imperialism in her own possessions, establish full democracy in India, and the Indian people must have the right of self-determination by framing their own constitution through a Constituent Assembly without external interference, and must guide their own policy. A free democratic India will gladly associate herself with other free nations for mutual defence against aggression and for economic cooperation. She will work for the establishment of a real world order based on freedom and democracy, utilizing the world's knowledge and resources for the progress and advancement of humanity.

The crisis that has overtaken Europe is not of Europe only but of humanity and will not pass like other crises or wars leaving the essential structure of the present-day world intact. It is likely to refashion the world for good or ill, politically, socially and economically. This crisis is the inevitable consequence of the social and political conflicts and contradictions which have grown alarmingly since the last Great War, and it will not be finally resolved till these conflicts and contradictions are removed and a new equilibrium established. That equilibrium can only be based on the ending of the domination and exploitation of one country by another, and on a reorganization of economic relations on a jouster basis for the common good of all. India is the crux of the problem, for India has been the outstanding example of modern imperialism and no refashioning of the world can succeed which ignores this vital problem. With her vast resources she must play an important part in any scheme of world reorganization. But she can only do so as a free nation whose energies have been released to work for this great end. Freedom today is inevitable and every attempt to retain imperialist domination in any part of the world will lead inevitably to fresh disaster.

The Working Committee have noted that many rulers of Indian States have offered their services and resources and expressed their desire to support the cause of democracy in Europe. If they must make their professions in favour of democracy abroad, the Committee would suggest that their first concern should be the introduction of democracy within their own States in which today undiluted autocracy reigns supreme. The British Government in India is more responsible for this autocracy than even the rulers themselves, as has been made painfully evident during the past year. This policy is the very negation of democracy and of the new world order for which Great Britain claims to be fighting in Europe.

As the Working Committee view past events in Europe, Africa and Asia, and more particularly past and present occurrences in India, they fail to find any attempt to advance the cause of democracy or self-determination or any evidence that the present war declarations of the British Government are being, or are going to be, acted upon. The true measure of democracy is the ending of Imperialism and Fascism alike and the aggression that has accompanied them in the past and the present. Only on that basis can a new order be built upon. In the struggle for that new world order, the Committee are eager and desirous to help in every way. But the Committee cannot associate themselves or offer any co-operation in a war which is meant to consolidate imperialism in India and elsewhere.

In view, however, of the gravity of the occasion and the fact that the pace of events during the last few days has often been swifter than the working of men's minds, the Committee desire to take no final decision at this stage, so as to allow for the full elucidation of the issues at stake, the real objectives aimed at, and the position of India in the present and the future. But the decision cannot be long delayed, as India is being committed from day-to-day to a policy to which she is not a party and of which she disapproves.

The Working Committee, therefore, invite the British Government to declare in unequivocal terms what their war aims are in regard to democracy and imperialism and the new order that is envisaged, in particular how these aims are going to apply to India and to be given effect to in the present. Do they include the elimination of imperialism and the treatment of India as a free nation whose policy will be guided in accordance with the wishes of her people? A clear declaration about the future, pledging the Government to the ending of Imperialism and Fascism alike, will be welcomed by the people of all countries, but it is far more important to give immediate effect to it to the largest possible extent, for only this will convince the people that the declaration is meant to be honoured. The real test of any declaration is its application in the present, for it is the present that will govern action today and give shape to the future.

War has broken out in Europe and the prospect is terrible to contemplate. But war has been taking its heavy toll of human life during recent years in Abyssinia, Spain and China. Innumerable innocent men, women and children have been bombed to death from the air in open cities, and cold-blooded massacres, torture and utmost humiliation have followed each other in quick succession during these years of horror. That horror grows, and violence and the threat of violence shadow the world and, unless checked and ended, will destroy the precious inheritance of past ages. That horror has to be checked in Europe and China, but it will not end till its root causes, Fascism and Imperialism, are removed. To that end the Working Committee are prepared to give their cooperation. But it will be infinite tragedy if even this terrible war is carried on in the spirit of imperialism and for the purpose of retaining this structure which is itself the cause of war and human degradation.

The Working Committee wish to declare that the Indian people have no quarrel with the German people or the Japanese people or any other people. But they have a deep-rooted quarrel with systems which deny freedom and are based on violence and aggression. They do not look forward to a victory of one people over another or to a dictated peace, but to a victory of real democracy for all the people of all countries and a world freed from the nightmare of violence and imperialist oppression.

The Committee earnestly appeal to the Indian people to end all internal conflict and controversy and, in this grave hour of peril, to keep in readiness and hold together as a united nation, clam of purpose and determined to achieve the freedom of India within a larger freedom of the world.

APPENDIX 3

Resolutions Adopted by Congress Working Committee,[1] *14 July 1942*

The events happening from day-to-day and the experience that the people of India are passing through confirm the opinion of Congressmen that British rule in India must end immediately, not merely because foreign domination even at its best is an evil in itself and a continuing injury to the subject people, but because India in bondage can play no effective part in defending herself and in affecting the fortunes of the war that is desolating humanity. The freedom of India is thus necessary not only in the interest of India, but also for the safety of the world and for the ending of Nazism, Fascism, militarism and other forms of imperialism, and the aggression of one nation over another. Ever since the outbreak of the World War, the Congress has studiedly pursued a policy of non-embarrassment. Even at the risk of making its satyagraha ineffective, it deliberately gave it a symbolic character in the hope that this policy of non-embarrassment carried to its logical extreme would be duly appreciated and that real power would be transferred to popular representatives so as to enable the nation to make its fullest contribution towards the realization of human freedom throughout the world, which is in danger of being crushed. It had also hoped that negatively nothing would be done which was calculated to tighten Britain's hold on India.

These hopes have, however, been dashed to pieces. The abortive Cripps proposals showed in the clearest possible manner that there was no change in the British Government's

[1] *Collected Works M.G.*, Vol. LXXVI (New Delhi, 1979), pp. 451–3.

attitude towards India and that the British hold on India was in no way to be relaxed. In the negotiations with Sir Stafford Cripps, Congress representatives tried their utmost to achieve a minimum, consistent with the national demand, but to no avail. This frustration has resulted in a rapid and widespread increase of ill-will against Britain and a growing satisfaction at the success of Japanese arms.

The Working Committee view this development with grave apprehension as this, unless checked, will inevitably lead to a passive acceptance of aggression. The Committee hold that all aggression must be resisted, for any submission to it must mean the degradation of the Indian people and the continuation of their subjection. The Congress is anxious to avoid the experience of Malaya, Singapore, and Burma and desires to build up resistance to any aggression or invasion of India by the Japanese or any other foreign power. The Congress would change the present ill-will against Britain into goodwill and make India a willing partner in a joint enterprise of securing freedom for the nations and peoples of the world and in the trials and tribulations which accompany it. This is only possible if India feels the glow of freedom.

The Congress representatives have tried their utmost to bring about a solution of the communal tangle. But this has been made impossible by the presence of the foreign power and only after the ending of foreign domination and intervention, can the present unreality give place to reality and the people of India, belonging to all groups and parties, face India's problems and solve them on a mutually agreed basis.

The present political parties formed chiefly with a view to attract the attention of and influence the British power, will then probably cease to function. For the first time in India's history, the realization will come home that the Princes, 'jagirdars', 'zamindars' and other propertied and moneyed classes derive their wealth and property from the workers in the fields and factories and elsewhere, to whom essentially power and authority must belong. On the withdrawal of British rule in India, responsible men and women of the country will come together to form a provisional government, representative of all important sections of the people of India which will later evolve a scheme by which a Constituent Assembly can be convened in order to prepare a Constitution for the Government of India acceptable to all sections of the people. Representatives of free India and representatives of Great Britain will confer together for the adjustment of future relations and for the cooperation of the two countries as allies in the common task of meeting aggression.

It is the earnest desire of the Congress to enable India to resist aggression effectively with the people's united will and strength behind it. In making the proposal for the withdrawal of the British rule from India, the Congress has no desire whatsoever to embarrass Great Britain or the Allied powers in their prosecution of the war, or in any way to encourage aggression on India or increase pressure on China by the Japanese or any other power associated with the Axis group. Nor does the Congress intend to jeopardize the defensive capacity of the Allied powers.

The Congress is, therefore, agreeable to the stationing of the armed forces of the Allies in India, should they so desire, in order to ward off and resist Japanese or any other aggression and to protect and help China. The proposal of withdrawal of the British power from India was never intended to mean the physical withdrawal of all Britishers from India, and certainly not of those who would make India their home and live there as citizens and as equals with the others. If such a withdrawal takes place with goodwill it would result in the establishing of a stable provisional government in India and cooperation between this government and the United Nations in resisting aggression and helping China. The Congress realizes that there may be risks involved in such a course. Such risks, however, have to be faced by any country in order to achieve freedom, and more especially in the present critical juncture in order to save the country and the larger cause of freedom the world over from far greater risks and perils. While, therefore, the Congress is impatient to achieve the national purpose it wishes to take no hasty steps and would like to avoid, in so far as possible any course of action that might embarrass the United Nations. The Congress would be pleased with the British power if it accepts the very reasonable and just proposal herein made not only in the interest of India but also that of Britain and of the cause of freedom, to which the United Nations proclaim their adherence. Should, however, this appeal fail the Congress cannot view without the gravest apprehension the continuation of the present state of affairs involving a progressive deterioration in the situation and the weakening of India's will and power to resist aggression. The Congress will then be reluctantly compelled to utilize all the non-violent strength it might have gathered since 1920 when it adopted non-violence as part of its policy for the vindication of the political rights and liberty. Such a widespread struggle would inevitable be under the leadership of Mahatma Gandhi. As issues raised are of the most vital and of far-reaching importance to the people of India as well as to the peoples of the United Nations the Working Committee refer them to the All-India Congress Committee for final decision. For this purpose the A.I.C.C. will meet in Bombay on the 7th August, 1942.

APPENDIX 4

'Quit India' Resolution Adopted by the All-India Congress Committee,[1] *8 August 1942*

The All-India Congress Committee has given the most careful consideration to the reference made to it by the Working Committee in their resolution dated July 14, 1942, and to subsequent events, including the development of the war situation, the utterances of responsible spokesmen of the British Government, and the comments and criticisms made in India and abroad. The Committee approves of and endorses that resolution, and is of opinion that events subsequent to it have given it further justification, and have made it clear that the immediate ending of British rule in India is an urgent necessity, both for the sake of India and for the success of the cause of the United Nations. The continuation of that rule is degrading and enfeebling India and making her progressively less capable of defending herself and of contributing to the cause of world freedom.

The Committee has viewed with dismay the deterioration of the situation on the Russian and Chinese fronts and conveys to the Russian and Chinese peoples its high appreciation of their heroism in defence of their freedom. This increasing peril makes it incumbent on all those who strive for freedom and who sympathize with the victims of aggression, to examine the foundations of the policy so far pursued by the Allied Nations, which have led to repeated and disastrous failures. It is not by adhering to such aims and policies and methods that failure can be converted into success, for past experience has shown that failure is inherent in them. These policies have

[1] *Collected Works M.G.*, Vol. LXXVI (New Delhi, 1979), pp. 458–61.

been based not on freedom so much as on the domination of subject and colonial countries and the continuation of the imperialist tradition and method. The possession of Empire, instead of adding to the strength of the ruling power, has become a burden and a curse. India, the classic land of modern Imperialism, has become the crux of the question, for by the freedom of India will Britain and the United Nations be judged, and the people of Asia and Africa be filled with hope and enthusiasm.

The ending of British rule in this country is thus a vital and immediate issue on which depend the future of the war and the success of freedom and democracy. A free India will assure this success by throwing all her resources in the struggle for freedom and against the aggression of Nazism, Fascism and Imperialism. This will not only affect materially the fortunes of the war, but will bring all subject and oppressed humanity on the side of the United Nations, and give these nations, whose ally India would be, the moral and spiritual leadership of the world. India in bondage will continue to be the symbol of British Imperialism and the taint of that Imperialism will affect the fortunes of all the United Nations.

The peril of today, therefore, necessitates the independence of India and the ending of British domination. No future promises or guarantees can affect the present situation or meet that peril. They cannot produce the needed psychological effect on the mind of the masses. Only the glow of freedom now can release that energy and enthusiasm of millions of people which will immediately transform the nature of the war.

The A.I.C.C., therefore, repeats with all emphasis the demand for the withdrawal of the British power from India. On the declaration of India's independence, a provisional government will be formed and free India will become an ally of the United Nations, sharing with them in the trials and tribulations of the joint enterprise of the struggle for freedom. The provisional government can only be formed by the cooperation of the principal parties and groups in the country. It will thus be a composite government, representative of all important sections of the people of India. Its primary functions must be to defend India and resist aggression with all the armed as well as the non-violent forces at its command, together with the Allied powers, and to promote the well-being and progress of the workers in the fields and factories and elsewhere, to whom essentially all power and authority must belong. The provisional government will evolve a scheme for a constituent assembly which will prepare a constitution for the government of India acceptable to all sections of the people. This constitution, according to the Congress view, should be a federal one, with the largest measure of autonomy for the federating units, and with the residuary powers vesting in these units. The future relations between India and the Allied nations will be adjusted by representatives of all these free countries conferring together for their mutual advantage and for their cooperation in the common task of resisting aggression. Freedom will enable India to resist aggression effectively with the people's united will and strength behind it.

The freedom of India must be the symbol of and prelude to the freedom of all other Asiatic nations under foreign domination. Burma, Malaya, Indo China, the Dutch Indies, Iran and Iraq must also attain their complete freedom. It must be clearly understood that such of these countries as are under Japanese control now must not subsequently be placed under the rule or control of any other colonial power.

While the A.I.C.C. must primarily be concerned with the independence and defence of India in this hour of danger, the Committee is of opinion that the future peace, security and ordered progress of the world demand a world federation of free nations, and on no other basis can the problems of the modern world be solved. Such a world federation would ensure the freedom of its constituent nations, the prevention of aggression and exploitation by one nation over another the protection of national minorities, the advancement of all backward areas and peoples and the pooling of the world's resources for the common good of all. On the establishment of such a world federation, disarmament would be practicable in all countries, national armies, navies and air forces would no longer be necessary, and a world federal defence force would keep the world peace and prevent aggression.

An independent India would gladly join such a world federation and cooperate on an equal basis with other countries in the solution of international problems.

Such a federation should be open to all nations who agree with its fundamental principles. In view of the war, however, the federation must inevitably, to begin with, be confined to the United Nations. Such a step taken will have a most powerful effect on the war, on the peoples of the Axis countries, and on the peace to come.

The Committee regretfully realizes, however, that despite the tragic and overwhelming lessons of the war and the perils that overhang the world, the governments of few countries are yet prepared to take this inevitable step towards world federation. The reactions of the British Government and the misguided criticisms of the foreign Press also make it clear that even the obvious demand for India's independence is resisted, though this has been made essentially to meet the present peril and to enable India to defend herself and help China and Russia in their hour of need. The Committee is anxious not to embarrass in any way the defence of China or

Russia whose freedom is precious and must be preserved, or to jeopardize the defensive capacity of the United Nations. But the peril grows both to India and to these nations, and inaction and submission to a foreign administration at this stage is not only degrading India and reducing her capacity to defend herself and resist aggression, but is no answer to that growing peril and is no service to the peoples of the United Nations. The earnest appeal of the Working Committee to Great Britain and the United Nations has so far met with no response, and the criticisms made in many foreign quarters have shown an ignorance of India's and the world's need, and sometimes even hostility to India's freedom, which is significant of a mentality of domination and racial superiority which cannot be tolerated by a proud people conscious of their strength and of the justice of their cause.

The A.I.C.C. would yet again, at this last moment, in the interest if world freedom, renew this appeal to Britain and the United Nations. But the Committee feels that it is no longer justified in holding the nation back from endeavouring to assert its will against an imperialist and authoritarian government, which dominates over and prevents it from functioning in its own interest and in the interest of humanity. The Committee resolves, therefore, to sanction, for the vindication of India's inalienable right to freedom and independence, the starting of a mass struggle on non-violent lines on the widest possible scale, so that the country might utilize all the non-violent strength it has gathered during the last twenty-two years of peaceful struggle. Such a struggle must inevitably be under the leadership of Gandhiji and the Committee requests him to take the lead and guide the nation in the steps to be taken.

The Committee appeals to the people of India to face the dangers and hardships that will fall to their lot with courage and endurance, and to hold together under the leadership of Gandhiji and carry out his instructions as disciplined soldiers of Indian freedom. They must remember that non-violence is the basis of this movement. A time may come when it may not be possible to issue instructions or for instructions to reach our people, and when no Congress committees can function. When this happens, every man and woman who is participating in this movement must function for himself or herself within the four corners of the general instructions issued. Every Indian who desires freedom and strives for it must be his own guide urging him on along the hard road where there is no resting place and which leads ultimately to the Independence and deliverance of India.

Lastly, whilst the A.I.C.C. has stated its own view of the future governance under free India the A.I.C.C. wishes to make it quite clear to all concerned that by embarking on mass struggle it has no intention of gaining power for the Congress. The power, when it comes, will belong to the whole people of India.

APPENDIX 5

AICC's Resolution Setting up the Objectives and Economic Programme Committee,[1] *15 June 1947*

Political independence having been achieved, the Congress must address itself to the next great task, namely, the establishment of real democracy in the country and a society based on social justice and equality. Such a society must provide every man and woman with equality of opportunity and freedom to work for the unfettered development of his or her personality. This can only be realized when democracy extends from the political to the social and the economic spheres. Democracy in the modern age necessitates planned central direction as well as decentralization of political and economic power, in so far as this is compatible with the safety of the State, with efficient production and the cultural progress of the community as a whole. The smallest territorial unit should be able to exercise effective control over its corporate life by means of a popularly elected Panchayat. In so far as it is possible, national and regional economic self-sufficiency in the essentials of life should be aimed at. In the case of industries, which in their nature must be run on a large-scale and on centralized basis, they should belong to the community, and they should be so organized that workers become not only co-sharers in profits but are also increasingly associated with the management and administration of the industry. Land with its mineral resources, and all other means of production, as well as distribution and exchange must belong to and be regulated by the community in its own interest.

[1] A.M. Zaidi and S.G. Zaidi, *The Encyclopaedia of the Indian National Congress*, Vol. 13 (New Delhi, 1981), pp. 120–1.

Our aim should be to evolve a political system which will combine efficiency of administration with individual liberty and an economic structure which will yield maximum production without the creation of private monopolies and the concentration of wealth and which will create proper balance between urban and rural economies. Such a social structure can provide an alternative to the acquisitive economy of private capitalism and the regimentation of a totalitarian state.

With a view to drawing up the economic programme for the Congress in accordance with above-mentioned principles and the election manifesto of the Congress dated December 19th 1945, the following Committee is appointed:

1. Pandit Jawaharlal Nehru, 2. Maulana Abul Kalam Azad, 3. Shri Jayaprakash Narayan, 4. Prof. N.G. Ranga, 5. Shri Gulzari Lal Nanda, 6. Shri J.C. Kumarappa, 7. Shri Achyut Patwardhan, 8. Shri Shankarrao Deo, with powers to coopt.

APPENDIX 6

The Light Has Gone Out[1]

Nehru's Broadcast to the Nation Announcing the Death of Mahatma Gandhi, 30 January 1948

Friends and comrades, the light has gone out of our lives and there is darkness everywhere. I do not know what to tell you and how to say it. Our beloved leader, Bapu as we called him, the Father of the Nation, is no more. Perhaps I am wrong to say that. Nevertheless, we will not see him again as we have seen him for these many years. We will not run to him for advice and seek solace from him, and that is a terrible blow, not to me only but to millions and millions in this country. And it is a little difficult to soften the blow by any other advice that I or anyone else can give you.

The light has gone out, I said, and yet I was wrong. For the light that shone in this country was no ordinary light. The light that has illumined this country for these many years will illumine this country for many more years, and a thousand years later, that light will still be seen in this country and the world will see it and it will give solace to innumerable hearts.

For that light represented something more than the immediate present; it represented the living, the eternal truths, reminding us of the right path, drawing us from error, taking this ancient country to freedom. All this has happened when there was so much more for him to do. We could never think that he was unnecessary or that he had done his task. But now, particularly, when we are faced with so many difficulties, his not being with us is a blow most terrible to bear.

[1] *Selected Works J.N.*, Vol. 5, second series (New Delhi, 1987), pp. 35–6.

A madman has put an end to his life, for I can only call him mad who did it and yet there has been enough of poison spread in this country during the past years and months, and this poison has had an effect on people's minds. We must face this poison, we must root out this poison, and we must face all the perils that encompass us, and face them not madly or badly, but rather in the way that our beloved teacher taught us to face them.

The first thing to remember now is that none of us dare misbehave because he is angry. We have to behave like strong and determined people, determined to face all the perils that surround us, determined to carry out the mandate that our great teacher and our great leader has given us, remembering always that if, as I believe, his spirit looks upon us and sees us, nothing would displease his soul so much as to see that we have indulged in any small misbehaviour or any violence. So we must not do that. But that does not mean that we should be weak, but rather that we should, in strength and in unity, face all the troubles that are in front of us. We must hold together, and all our petty troubles and difficulties and conflicts must be ended in the face of this great disaster. A great disaster is a symbol to us to remember all the big things of life and forget the small things of which we have thought too much. In his death he has reminded us of the big things of life, the living truth, and if we remember that, then it will be well with India. It was proposed by some friends that Mahatmaji's body should be embalmed for a few days to enable millions of people to pay their last homage to him. But it was his wish, repeatedly expressed, that no such thing should happen, that this should not be done, that he was entirely opposed to any embalming of his body, and so we decided that we must follow his wishes in this matter, however, much others might have wished otherwise.

And so the cremation will take place on Saturday in Delhi city by the side of the Jumna River. On Saturday forenoon, about 11–30, the pier will be taken out at Birla House and it will follow a prescribed route and go to the Jumna River. The cremation will take place there at about 4 p.m. The place and route will be announced by radio and the Press.

People in Delhi who wish to pay their last homage should gather along this route. I will not advise too many of them to come to Birla House, but rather to gather on both sides of this long route from Birla House to the Jumna River. And I trust that they will remain there in silence without any demonstrations. That is the best way and the most fitting way to pay homage to this great soul. Also, Saturday should be a day of fasting and prayer for all of us.

Those who live elsewhere, out of Delhi and in other parts of India, will no doubt also take such part as they can in this last homage. For them also, let this be a day of fasting and prayer. And at the appointed time for cremation, that is 4 p.m. on Saturday afternoon, people should go to the river or to the sea and offer prayers there. And while we pray, the greatest prayer that we can offer is to take a pledge to dedicate ourselves to the truth, and to the cause for which this great countryman of ours lived and for which he has died. That is the best prayer that we can offer him and his memory. That is the best prayer that we can offer to India and ourselves. *Jai Hind.*

APPENDIX 7

A Glory that is No More[1]

Nehru's Speech in the Constituent Assembly (Legislative), 2 February 1948

Sir, may I associate myself with what you have said? It is customary in this house to pay some tribute to the eminent departed, to say some words of praise and condolence. I am not quite sure in my own mind if it is exactly fitting for me or for any others of this House to say much on this occasion, for I have a sense of utter shame both as an individual and as the head of the Government of India that we should have failed to protect the greatest treasure that we possessed. It is our failure, as it has been our failure in the many month past, to give protection to many an innocent man, woman and child; it may be that the burden and the task was too great for us or for any Government. Nevertheless, it is a failure. And today the fact that this mighty person whom we honoured and loved beyond measure has gone because we could not give him adequate protection is a shame for all of us. It is a shame to me as an Indian that an Indian should have raised his hand against him, it is a shame to me as a Hindu that a Hindu should have done this deed and done it to the greatest Indian of the day and the greatest Hindu of the age.

We praise people in well-chosen words and we have some kind of a measure for greatness. How shall we praise him and how shall we measure him, because he was not of the common clay that all of us are made of? He came, lived a fairly long span of life, and has passed away. No words of praise of

[1] *Selected Works J.N.*, Vol. 5, second series (New Delhi, 1987), pp. 39–42.

ours in this House are needed, for he has had greater praise in his life than any living man in history. And during these two or three days sine his death he has had the homage of the world; what can we add to that? How can we praise him, how can we who have been children of his, and perhaps more intimately his children than the children of his body, for we have all been in some greater or smaller measure the children of his spirit, unworthy as we were?

A glory has departed and the sun that warmed and brightened our lives has set and we shiver in the cold and dark. Yet, he would not have us feel this way. After all, that glory that we saw for all these years, that man with the divine fire, changed us also—and such as we are, we have been moulded by him during these years, that man with the divine fire, changed us also—and such as we are, we have been moulded by him during these years; and out of that divine fire many of us also took a small spark which strengthened and made us work to some extent on the lines that he fashioned. And so if we praise him, our words seem rather small, and if we praise him, to some extent we also praise ourselves. Great men and eminent men have monuments in bronze and marble set up for them, but this man of divine fire managed in his lifetime to become enshrined in millions and millions of hearts so that all of us became somewhat of the stuff that he was made of, though to an infinitely lesser degree. He spread out in this way all over India, not in palaces only, or in select places or in assemblies, but in every hamlet and hut of the lowly and those who suffer. He lives in the hearts of millions and he will live for immemorial ages.

What then can we say about him except to feel humble on this occasion? To praise him we are not worthy—to praise him whom we could not follow adequately and sufficiently. It is almost doing him an injustice just to pass him by with words when he demanded work and labour and sacrifice from us; in a large measure he made this country, during the last thirty years or more, attain to heights of sacrifice which in that particular domain have never been equalled elsewhere. He succeeded in that. Yet ultimately things happened which do doubt made him suffer tremendously though his tender face never lost its smile and he never spoke a harsh word to anyone. Yet, he must have suffered—suffered for the failing of this generation whom he had trained, suffered because we went away from the path that he had shown us. And ultimately the hand of a child of his—for he, after all, is as much a child of his as any other Indian—a hand of that child of his struck him down.

Long ages afterwards history will judge of this period that we have passed through. It will judge of the successes and the failures. We are too near it to be proper judges, and to understand what has happened and what has not happened. All we know is that there was a glory and that it is no more; all we know is that for the moment there is darkness, not so dark certainly, because when we look into our hearts we still find the living flame which he lighted there. And if those living flames exist, there will not be darkness in this land and we shall be able, with our effort, remembering him and following his path, to illumine this land again, small as we are, but still with the fire that he instilled into us.

He was perhaps the greatest symbol of the India of the past, and, may I say, of the India of the future, that we could have had. We stand on this perilous edge of the present between that past and the future to be, and we face all manner of perils and the greatest peril is sometimes the lack of faith which comes to us, the sense of frustration that comes to us, the sinking of the heart and of the spirit that comes to us when we see ideals go over-board, when we see the great things that we talked about somehow pass into empty words and life takes a different course. Yet, I do believe that perhaps this period will pass soon enough.

Great as this man of God was in his life, he was been great in his death and I have not the shadow of a doubt that by his death he has served the great cause as he served it throughout his life. We mourn him; we shall always mourn him, because we are human and cannot forget our beloved Master. But I know that he would not like us to mourn him. No tears came to his eyes when his dearest and closest passed away—only a firm resolve to persevere, to serve the great cause that he had chosen. So he would chide us if we merely mourn. That is a poor way of doing homage to him. The only way is to express our determination, to pledge ourselves anew, to conduct ourselves in a befitting manner and to dedicate ourselves to the great task which he undertook and which he accomplished to such a large extent. So we have to work, we have to labour, we have to sacrifice and thus prove, to some extent at least, worthy followers of his.

It is clear, as you said, Sir, that this happening, this tragedy, is not merely an isolated act of a madman. This comes out of a certain atmosphere of violence and hatred that has prevailed in this country for many months and years and more especially in the past few months. That atmosphere envelops us and surrounds us and if we are to serve the cause he put before us, we have to face this atmosphere, to combat it, to struggle against it and root out the evil of hatred and violence.

So far as this Government is concerned, I trust they will spare no means, spare no effort to tackle it, because if we do not do that, if we, in our weakness or for any other reason that we may consider adequate, do not adopt effective means to stop this violence, to stop this spreading of hatred by word of mouth or writing or act, then indeed we are not worthy of being in this Government; we are certainly not worthy of being his followers and we are not worthy of even saying words of praise for this great soul who has departed. So on this occasion or any other when we think of this great Master who has gone, let us always think of him in terms of work and labour and sacrifice, in terms of fighting evil wherever we see it, in terms of holding to the truth as he put it before us, and if we do so, however, unworthy we may be, we shall at least have done our duty and paid proper homage to his spirit.

He has gone, and all over India there is a feeling of having been left desolate and forlorn. All of us sense that feeling, and I do not know when we shall be able to get rid of it, and yet together with that feeling there is also a feeling of proud thankfulness that it has been given to us of this generation to be associated with this mighty person. In ages to come, centuries and may be millennia after us, people will think of this generation when this man of God trod on earth and will think of us who, however small, could also follow his path and tread the holy ground where his feet had been. Let us be worthy of him.

APPENDIX 8

The Last Journey,[1] *12 February 1948*

The last journey has ended. The final pilgrimage has been made. For over fifty years Mahatma Gandhi wandered all over our great country from the Himalayas and the North West Frontier and the Brahmaputra in the north-east to Kanyakumari in the far south. He visited every part of the country, not for pleasure but to understand and serve the people. Perhaps no other Indian has travelled so extensively in the country or got to know and served her people so well. And now his journey in this world is over, though we have still to go a long way. Some grieve over his passing away, and this is natural and proper. But why should we grieve? Do we grieve for him or for something else? In his life, as in his death, he lent a radiance to our country which will keep it always illumined. Why then should we grieve for him? Yes, we rather grieve for ourselves for our own weaknesses, for the ill-will in our hearts, for our conflicts with others. We have to remember that it was to remove all these that Mahatma Gandhi sacrificed his life. It was this problem which had gripped him during these last few months. We honour him not for his name alone, but for what he stood for, what he taught us, and especially what he died for.

Let us, standing here on the banks of the Ganga, at the Triveni, search our own hearts and ask ourselves the question: how far have we done our duty, how far have we followed his path, how far have we tried to live in peace and

[1] Speech on the occasion of the immersion of Mahatma Gandhi's ashes at Triveni, the confluence of three rivers—Ganga, Jamuna and Saraswati—at Allahabad, 12 February 1948. A.I.R. tapes, N.M.M.L. (Original in Hindi). *Selected Works J.N.*, Vol. 5, second series (New Delhi, 1987), pp. 53–7.

cooperation with others? If we think about this and even, now we follow the right path, it will be well with us and well with our country.

Our country gave birth to a great man. He shone like a beacon not only for our country but for the whole world. And yet he was done to death by one of our own brothers. How did this happen? You might think that it was an act of madness. But that does not explain this tragedy. It could only occur because a seed of poison had been sown in our hearts against one another—a poison of enmity and hatred—and such acts affected the country and affected so many of our people. Now it is our duty to put an end to this poison of hatred and ill-will. If we have learnt anything from the Mahatma, we must bear no enmity towards any person. An individual is not our enemy. It is the poison within him that we must fight and root out. We are weak but Gandhiji's strength passed into us and we have acquired some stature, living in his shadow. In his reflected glory we seemed to have acquired some strength. But the real strength and glory were his and the path he showed was also his. We stumbled often enough and fell down in our attempts to tread that path and so could do some service to the country.

Now our pillar of strength and support is no more. But how can I say this? There are lakhs here and millions in the country in whose hearts the Mahatma's image is enshrined. Future generations of our people, who have not seen him or heard him, will also have that image in their hearts because that image is now a part of India's inheritance and history.

The Gandhian era, which began thirty or forty years ago in India, has, in a sense, come to an end today. And yet I am wrong, for it has not ended. Perhaps it is, in a way, just beginning. Thus far we have been leaning on him for advice and support; from now onwards we have to stand on our own feet, taking, of course, the support of his teachings, and rely on ourselves. May his memory and his teachings light our path? Remember his last lesson, his message, which was that we should be free from fear. He taught us constantly to root out all fear and enmity from our hearts, live in peace with one another and keep our country free.

He led our country to freedom and the world marvelled at the way he did it. But at the very moment of gaining our freedom we forgot his lesson. We were misled. We fought with one another and disgraced our country. Many of our youths shouted all kinds of slogans and took to the wrong path. Are we to drive them away and crush them? But they are still our own people and we have to win them over.

I want to tell you that this communal poison which keeps Hindus against Muslims and Muslims against Hindus or Sikhs, whether it springs from religious fervour or in the name of religion, it will end our freedom if we are not vigilant. It was to awaken us to this impending danger that Gandhiji undertook his last fast two or three weeks ago. This aroused the nation's conscience and we and other representatives of the people pledged to behave better. It was only then that he gave up his fast. Gandhiji used to observe silence for one day in every week. Who knew that an unending silence and fasting were to begin now that his voice is silenced for ever.

His last lesson was that of putting an end to all this fighting and killing and we must keep this lesson in mind. For his assassination is a grim warning of what can happen. Why was such a great man murdered? It was because some people did into agree with him politically. This is a most dangerous path. For Swaraj means that we should try to understand one another and work by persuasion. People should choose their representatives and their decisions should be implemented. If we do not work by persuasion but use violence against one another, then the very nation gets destroyed.

I see many soldiers of the Indian Army in the audience. It is their duty to defend their country. If they were to quarrel among themselves, what would their strength be worth and how could they serve their country? True Swaraj demands mutual consultation and harmonious living.

Democracy demands discipline, tolerance and mutual regard. Freedom demands respect for the freedom of others. In a democracy changes are made by mutual discussion and persuasion and not by violent means. If a government has no popular support, another government which commands that popular support takes its place. It is only small groups who know that they cannot get sufficient popular support that resort to methods of violence, imagining in their folly that they can gain their ends in this way. This is not only utterly wrong but it is also quite foolish. For the reaction to the violence of the minority, which seeks to coerce the majority, is to provoke the majority into violence against it.

This great tragedy has happened because many persons, including some in high places, have poisoned the atmosphere of this country of ours. It is the duty of the Government as well as the people to root out this poison. We have had our lesson at a terrible cost. Is there anyone amongst us now who will not pledge himself after Gandhiji's death to fulfil his mission a mission for which the greatest man of our country, the greatest man in the world, has laid down his life?

And now you and I and all of us will go back from the banks of the Ganga. We shall feel sad and lonely. We shall never see Gandhiji again. We used to run to him for advice and guidance whenever we faced any great problems or were in doubt or disturbed. There is no one to give us advice now or to share our burdens. It is not I alone or a few of us who looked up to him for help. Millions of our countrymen considered him a friend. We went to him as though we were his children. Rightly did he come to be known as the Father of the Nation. In millions of homes in the country today there is mourning as on the passing away of a beloved father.

We shall go away from here, sad and lonely, but with a sense of pride because of the realization that our country produced such a noble personality. He led our country to great heights along a unique path to freedom and truth. The path he showed us was one of fighting for the good. It is not the way of sitting quietly on a Himalayan peak. He was always ready to fight for right causes. But his battle was one of truth, non-violence and peace—and yet it was a battle by which he set forty crores of people free. We cannot, therefore, remain passive. We have our obligations to fulfil and the duty to perform to which we have pledged ourselves. That duty is to eradicate this poison, follow the path of truth, and build such a free country, where all individuals of every faith, can live in harmony. It should be a country which will set an example to the rest of the world. If we take this pledge we shall have learnt a great lesson. If we fail, it will be said that a great man came among us but the people were not worthy of him, they could not understand his greatness.

How often, in the last thirty or forty years, we have shouted *Mahatma Gandhi ki jai*! Yet it hurt Gandhiji to hear that slogan. What victory could we wish him? He was already the victorious one. It is you and I, and this unfortunate country, who have still to struggle for victory. Even a thousand years hence people will remember him because he was the victorious one. He desired my and your victory. To raise the people of this country, especially the poor, the downtrodden, the kisans and our Harijan brothers, was the mission of his life. In working for them he adopted their ways of life and dress which were in accord with the lifestyle of the weak and the poor people. He often spoke of *Daridranarayan.* It was in this way that he worked for the victory of the people. No one can give us this victory. We have to work for it through our own efforts. He taught us the way to triumph. He taught us the kind of triumph that he wished for us—not the superficial triumph for which most people and countries strive through violence, treachery and evil means. That kind of victory is always short-lived. Gandhiji wanted a victory that would rest on the foundation of truth which, no matter how high we built the structure upon it, would not collapse. Today the world is in a state of political flux—some countries are rising, others are going down. Untruth, turmoil and deceit characterize the politics of the world today. Gandhiji taught us a different kind of method—a new method of struggle and warfare. He demonstrated the efficacy of truth, of non-violence and of living for one another. He taught us to respect the many religions which have been in this country for a long time and are not foreign. We all belong to India, and we are all brothers and sisters and must live in harmony. We are all equal partners in the freedom that we have won. We have no right to encroach on the rights of others or to deprive others of their share. All Indian—30 or 40 crores—should have an equal right to opportunities and blessings that free India has to offer. We do not want a handful of rich men to take the major share and leave the rest of the people poor. This was not the Swaraj that the Mahatma envisaged. It is not easy to achieve that Swaraj for the people but we are slowly striving in that direction, drawing sometimes upon Gandhiji's teachings and supported by his strength and ideal.

Now, with his last lesson in mind, we must strive for the same ideal more vigorously, destroying all evils in the path. Only then can we in truth and honesty, be worthy to say *Mahatma Gandhi ki jai*!

APPENDIX 9

The Perfect Artist[1]

Written by Nehru on 5 February 1948 and Published in *Harijan*, 15 February 1948

Nineteen-sixteen. Over thirty-two years ago. That was when I first saw Bapu, and an age has gone by since then. Inevitably one looks back and memories crowd in. What a strange period this has been in India's history and the story, with all its ups and downs and triumphs and defeats, has the quality of a ballad and a romance. Even our trivial lives were touched by a halo of romance, because we lived through this period and were actors, in greater or lesser degree, in the great drama of India.

This period has been full of wars and upheavals and stirring events all over the world. Yet events in India stand out in a distinctive outline because they were on an entirely different plane. If a person studied this period without knowing much of Bapu he would wonder how and why all this happened in India. It is difficult to explain it; it is even difficult to understand by the cold light of reason why each one of us behaved as he or she did. It sometimes happens that an individual or even a nation is swept away by some gust of emotion or feeling into a particular type of action, sometimes noble action, more often ignoble action. But that passion and feeling pass and the individual soon returns to his normal levels of action and inaction.

The surprising thing about India during this period was not only that the country as a whole functioned on a high

[1] *Selected Works J.N.*, Vol. 5, second series (New Delhi, 1987), pp. 48–9.

plane, but also that it functioned more or less continuously for a lengthy period on that plane. That indeed was a remarkable achievement. It cannot easily be explained or understood unless one looks upon the astonishing personality that moulded this period. Like a colossus he stands astride half a century of India's history, a colossus not of the body but of the mind and spirit.

We mourn for Bapu and feel orphaned. Looking back at his magnificent life, what is there to mourn for? Surely to very, very few human beings in history could it have been given to find so much fulfilments in their own lives. He was sad for our failures and unhappy at not having raised India to greater heights. That sadness and unhappiness are easy to understand. Yet who dare say that his life was a failure? Whatever he touched he turned into something worthwhile and precious. Whatever he did yielded substantial results, though perhaps not as great as he hoped for. One carried away the impression that he could not really fail in anything that he attempted. According to the teachings of the *Gita*, he laboured dispassionately without caring too much for results, and so results came to him.

During his long life, full of hard work and activity and novel adventures out of the common rut, there is hardly any jarring note anywhere. All his manifold activities became progressively a symphony and every word he spoke and every gesture that he made fitted into this and so unconsciously he became the perfect artist for he had learnt the art of living, though the way of life he had adopted was very different from the world's way. It became apparent that the pursuit of truth and goodness leads among other things to this artistry in life.

As he grew older his body seemed to be just a vehicle for

the mighty spirit within him. Almost one forgot the body as one listened to him or looked at him, and so where he sat became a temple and where he trod was hollowed ground.

Even in his death there was a magnificence and complete artistry. It was from every point of view a fitting climax to the man and to the life he had lived. Indeed, it heightened the lesson of his life. He died in the fullness of his powers and, as he would no doubt have liked to die, at the moment of prayer. He died a martyr to the cause of unity to which he had always been devoted and for which he had worked unceasingly, more specially during the past year or more. He died suddenly as all men should wish to die. There was no fading away of the body or a long illness or the forgetfulness of the mind that comes with age. Why then should we grieve for him? Our memories of him will be of the Master, whose step was light to the end, whose smile was infectious and whose eyes where full of laughter. We shall associate no tailing powers with him of body or mind. He lived and he died at the top of his strength and powers, leaving a picture in our minds and in the mind of the age that we live in that can never fade away.

That picture will not fade. But he did something much more than that, for he entered into the very stuff of our minds and spirits and changed them and moulded them. The Gandhi generation will pass away, but that stuff will remain and will affect each succeeding generation, for it has become a part of India's spirit. Just when we were growing poor in the spirit in this country, Bapu came to enrich us and make us strong, and the strength he gave us was not for a moment or a day or a year but it was something added on to our national inheritance.

Bapu has done a giant's work for India and the world and

even for our poor selves, and he has done it astonishingly well. And now it is our turn not fail him or his memory but to carry on the work to the best of our ability and to fulfil the pledges we have so often taken.

APPENDIX 10

Nehru's Reminiscenses of Gandhi (1949)[1]

While India was politically dormant in the pre-war years [before 1914], a far country saw a gallant and unique struggle for India's honour. This was South Africa, where large numbers of Indian labourers and some merchants had emigrated. They were humiliated and ill-treated in a host of ways, for racial arrogance reigned supreme there. It so happened that a young Indian barrister was taken to South Africa to appear in a law case. He was the condition of his fellow countrymen, and he was humiliated and distressed by it. He resolved to do his best to help them. For many years he laboured quietly, giving up his profession and his belongings and devoting himself entirely to the cause he had espoused.

This man was Mohandas Karamchand Gandhi. Today every child in India knows him and loves him, but then he was little known outside South Africa. Suddenly his name flashed across to India, and people talked of him and of his brave fight with surprise and admiration and pride. The South African government had tried to humiliate the Indian residents there still more, and under Gandhiji's leadership they had refused to submit. This was strange enough, that a community of poor, downtrodden, ignorant workers and a group of petty merchants, far from their home country, should take up this brave attitude.

What was stranger still was the method they had adopted, for as a political weapon this was a novel one in the world's history. We have heard of it often enough since. It was Gandhiji's *satyagraha*, which means holding on to truth. It is

[1] Jawaharlal Nehru, *Mahatma Gandhi* (Bombay, 1949), pp. 9–37.

sometimes called passive resistance, but that is not a correct translation, for it is active enough. It is not non-resistance merely, though *ahimsa* or non-violence is an essential part of it. Gandhiji startled India and South Africa with this non-violence warfare, and people in India learned with a thrill of pride and joy of the thousands of our countrymen and women who went willingly to jail in South Africa. In our hearts we were ashamed of our subjection and our impotence in our own country, and this instance of a brave challenge on behalf of our own people increased our own self-respect. Suddenly India became politically awake on this issue, and money poured into South Africa. The fight was stopped when Gandhiji and the South African government came to terms.

First Meeting

My first meeting with Gandhiji was about the time of the Lucknow Congress during Christmas 1916. All of us admired him for his heroic fight in South Africa, but he seemed very distant and different and unpolitical to many of us young men. He refused to take part in Congress or national politics then and confined himself to the South African Indian question. Soon afterward his adventures and victory in Champaran, on behalf of the tenants of the planters, filled us with enthusiasm. We saw that he was prepared to apply him methods in India also, and they promised success.

The New Voice

India waited after the war; resentful, rather aggressive, not very hopeful, but still expectant. Within a few months, the first fruits of the new British policy, so eagerly waited for, appeared in the shape of a proposal to pass special laws to control the revolutionary movement. Instead of more freedom, there was to be more repression. These bills were based on the report of a committee and were known as the Rowlatt Bills. But very soon they were called the 'Black Bills' all over the country, and were denounced everywhere and by every Indian, including even the most moderate. They gave great powers to the government and the police to arrest, keep in prison without trial, or to have a secret trial of any person they disapproved of or suspected. A famous description of these bills at the time was: *na vakil, na appeal, na dalil.* As the outcry against the bills gained volume, a new factor appeared, a little cloud on the political horizon which grew and spread rapidly till it covered the Indian sky.

This new factor was Mohandas Karamchand Gandhi. He had returned to India from South Africa during wartime and settled down with his colony in an ashrama in Sabarmati. He had kept away from politics. He had even helped the government in recruiting men for the war. He was, of course, very well known in India since his *Satyagraha* struggle in South Africa. In 1917 he had championed with success the miserable downtrodden tenants of the European planters in the Champaran district of Bihar. Later he had stood up for the peasantry of Kaira in Gujrat. Early in 1919 he was very ill. He had barely recovered the Rowlatt Bill agitation filled the country. He also joined his voice to the universal outcry.

But this voice was somehow different from the others. It was quiet and low, and yet it could be heard above the shouting of the multitude; it was soft and gentle, and yet there seemed to be steel hidden away somewhere in it; it was courteous and full of appeal, and yet there was something grim and frightening in it; every word used was full of meaning and seemed to carry a deadly earnestness. Behind the language of peace and friendship there was power and the quivering shadow of action and a determination not to submit to a wrong. We are familiar with that voice now; we have heard it often enough during the last fourteen years. But it was new to us in February and March 1919; we did not quite know what to make of it, but we were thrilled. This was something very different from our noisy politics of condemnation and nothing else, long speeches always ending in the same futile and ineffective resolutions of protest which nobody took very seriously. This was the politics of action, not of talk.

The Satyagraha Movement

Gandhiji had passed through a serious illness early in 1919. Almost from his sick bed be begged the Viceroy not to give his consent to the Rowlatt Bills. That appeal was ignored as others had been and then, almost against his will, Gandhiji took the leadership in his first all-India agitation. He started the Satyagraha Sabha, the members of which were pledged to disobey the Rowlatt Act, if it was applied to them, as well as other objectionable laws to be specified from time to time. In other words they were to court gaol openly and deliberately.

When I first read about this proposal in the newspapers my reaction was one of tremendous relief. Here at last was a way out of the tangle, a method of action which was straight and open and possibly effective. I was afire with enthusiasm and wanted to join the Satyagraha Sabha immediately. I hardly thought of the consequences—law-breaking, gaol-going, etc. —and if I thought of them I did not care. But suddenly my ardour was damped and I realized that all was not plain sailing. My father was dead against this new idea. He was not in the habit of being swept away by new proposals; he thought carefully of the consequences before he took any fresh step. And the more he thought of the Satyagraha Sabha and its programme, the less he liked it. What good would the gaol-going of a number of individuals do, what pressure could it bring on the Government? Apart from these general considerations, what really moved him was the personal issue. It seemed to him preposterous that I should go to prison. The trek to prison had not then begun and the idea was most repulsive. Father was intensely attached to his children. He was not showy in his affection, but behind his restraint there was a great love.

For many days there was this mental conflict, and because both of us felt that big issues were at stake involving a complete upsetting of our lives, we tried hard to be as considerate to each other as possible. I wanted to lessen his obvious suffering if I could, but I had no doubt in my mind that I had to go the way of *Satyagraha.* Both of us had a distressing time, and night after night I wandered about alone, tortured in mind and trying to grope my way out. Father—I discovered later—actually tried sleeping on the floor to find out what it was like, as he thought that this would be my lot in prison.

Gandhiji came to Allahabad at father's request and they had long talks at which I was not present. As a result Gandhiji advised me not to precipitate matters or to do anything which might upset father. I was not happy at this, but other events took place in India which changed the whole situation, and the Satyagraha Sabha stopped its activities.

Satyagraha Day—all-India *hartals* and complete suspension of business firing by the police and military at Delhi and Amritsar, and the killing of many people—mob violence in Amritsar and Ahmedabad—the massacre of Jallianwala Bagh—the long horror and terrible indignity of martial law in the Punjab. The Punjab was isolated, cut-off from the rest of India; a thick veil seemed to cover it and hide it from outside eyes. There was hardly any news, and people could not go there or come out from there.

Odd individuals, who managed to escape from that inferno, were so terror-struck that they could give no clear account. Helplessly and impotently, we, who were outside, waited for scraps of news and bitterness filled our hearts. Some of us wanted to go openly to the affected parts of the Punjab and defy the martial law regulations. But we were kept back, and meanwhile a big organization for relief and enquiry was set up on behalf of the Congress.

As soon as martial law was withdrawn from the principal areas and outsiders were allowed to come in, prominent Congressmen and others poured into the Punjab offering their services for relief or enquiry work. The relief work was largely directed by Pandit Madan Mohan Malaviya and Swami Shraddhananda; the enquiry part was mainly under the direction of my father and Mr. C.R. Das, with Gandhiji taking a great deal of interest in it and often being consulted by the others. Deshbandhu Das especially took the Amritsar area under his charge and I was deputed to accompany him there and assist him in any way he desired. That was the first occasion I had of working with him and under him and I valued that experience very much and my admiration for him grew. Most of the evidence relating to Jallianwala Bagh and that terrible lane where human beings were made to crawl on their bellies, that subsequently appeared in the Congress Inquiry Report, was taken down in our presence. We paid numerous visits to the so-called Bagh itself and examined every bit of it carefully.

During the Punjab inquiry I saw a great deal of Gandhiji. Very often his proposals seemed novel to our committee and it did not approve of them. But almost always he argued his way to their acceptance and subsequent events showed the wisdom of his advice. Faith in his political insight grew in me.

The First Gandhi Congress

The Amritsar Congress was the first Gandhi Congress. Lokamanya Tilak was also present and took a prominent part in the deliberations, but there could be no doubt about it that the majority of the delegates, and even more so the great crowds outside, looked to Gandhiji for leadership. The slogan *Mahatma Gandhi ki jai* began to dominate the Indian political horizon. The Ali Brothers, recently discharged from internment, immediately joined the Congress, and the national movement began to take a new shape and develop a new orientation.

M. Mohammad Ali went off soon on a Khilafat deputation to Europe. In India the Khilafat Committee came more and more under Gandhiji's influence and began to flirt with his ideas of non-violent non-cooperation. I remember one of the earliest meetings of the Khilafat leaders and Moulvies and Ulemas in Delhi in January 1920. A Khilafat deputation was going to wait on the Viceroy, and Gandhiji was to join it. Before he reached Delhi, however, a draft of the proposed address was, according to custom, sent to the Viceroy. When Gandhiji arrived and read this draft, he strongly disapproved of it and even said that he could not be a party to the deputation, if this draft was not materially altered. His objection was that the draft was vague and wordy and there was no clear indication in it of the absolute minimum demands which the Muslims must have. He said that this was not fair to the Viceroy and the British Government, or to the people, or to themselves. They must not make exaggerated demands which they were not going to press, but should state the minimum clearly and without possibility of doubt, and stand by it to the death. If they were serious, this was only right and honourable course to adopt.

This argument was a novel one in political or other circles in India. We were used to vague exaggerations and flowery language and always there was an idea of a bargain in our minds. Gandhiji, however, carried his point and he wrote to the Private Secretary of the Viceroy, pointing out the defects and vagueness of the draft address sent, and forwarding a few additional paragraphs to be added to it. These paragraphs gave the minimum demands. The Viceroy's reply was interesting. He refused to accept the new paragraphs and said that the previous draft was, in his opinion, quite proper. Gandhiji felt that this correspondence had made his own position and that of the Khilafat Committee clear, and so he joined the deputation after all.

It was obvious that the Government were not going to accept the demands of the Khilafat Committee and struggle was therefore bound to come. There were long talks with the Moulvies and the Ulemas, and non-violence and non-cooperation were discussed, especially non-violence Gandhiji told them that he was theirs to command, but on the definite understanding that they accepted non-violence with all its implications. There was to be no weakening on that, no temporizing, no mental reservations. It was not easy for the Moulvies to grasp this idea but they agreed, making it clear that they did so as a policy only and not as a creed, for their religion did not prohibit the use of violence in a righteous cause.

Gandhiji and the Khilafat Movement

The political and the Khilafat movement developed side by side during that year 1920, both going in the same direction and eventually joining hands with the adoption by the Congress of Gandhiji's non-violent non-cooperation. The Khilafat Committee adopted this programme first, and August 1st was fixed for the commencement of the campaign.

Earlier in the year a Muslim meeting (I think it was the Council of the Moslem League) was held in Allahabad to consider this programme. The meeting took place in Syed Raza Ali's house. M. Mohammad Ali was still in Europe but M. Shaukat Ali was present. I remember that meeting because it thoroughly disappointed me. Shaukat Ali was, of course, full of enthusiasm but almost all the others looked thoroughly unhappy and uncomfortable. They did not have the courage to disagree and yet they obviously had no intention of doing anything rash. Were these the people to lead a revolutionary movement, I thought, and to challenge the British Empire? Gandhiji addressed them and after hearing him they looked even more frightened than before. He spoke well in his best dictatorial vein. He was humble but also clear-cut and hard as a diamond, pleasant and soft-spoken but inflexible and terribly earnest. His eyes were mild and deep, yet out of them blazed out a fierce energy and determination. This is going to be a great struggle, he said, with a very powerful adversary. If you want to take it up, you must be prepared to lose everything, and you must subject yourself to the strictest non-violence and discipline. When war is declared martial law prevails, and in our non-violent struggle there will also have to be dictatorship and martial law on our side, if we are to win. You have every right to kick me out, to demand my head, or to punish me whenever and, howsoever, you choose. But so long as you choose to keep me as your leader you must accept my conditions, you must accept dictatorship and the discipline of martial law. But that dictatorship will always be subject to your goodwill and to your acceptance and to your cooperation. The moment you have had enough of me, throw me out, trample upon me, and I shall not complain.

Something to this effect he said and these military analogies and the unyielding earnestness of the man made the flesh of most of his hearers creep. But Shaukat Ali was there to keep the waverers up to the mark, and when the time for voting came the great majority of them quietly and shamefacedly voted for the proposition, that is for war!

As we were coming home from the meeting. I asked Gandhiji if this was the way to start a great struggle. I had expected enthusiasm, spirited language and a flashing of eyes; instead we saw a very tame gathering of timid, middle-aged folk. And yet these people, such was the pressure of mass opinion, voted for the struggle. Of course, very few of these members of the Moslem League joined the struggle later. Many of them found a safe sanctuary in Government jobs. The Moslem League did not represent, then or later, any considerable section of Moslem opinion. It was the Khilafat Committee of 1920 that was a powerful and far more representative body, and it was this Committee that entered upon the struggle with enthusiasm. . . .

Congress Takes the Plunge

The next year the Congress took the plunge, and adopted Gandhiji's programme of non-cooperation. A special session in Calcutta adopted this, and later the annual session in Nagpur confirmed it. The method of struggle was a perfectly peaceful one, non-violent as it was called, and its basis was a refusal to help the government in its administration and exploitation of India. To begin with there were to be a number of boycotts—of titles given by the foreign government, of official functions and the like, of law courts by both lawyers and litigants, of official schools and colleges, and of the new councils under the Montagu-Chelmsford reforms. Later the boycotts were to extend to the civil and military services and the payment of taxes. On the constructive side stress was laid on hand spinning and the *khaddar*, and on arbitration courts to take the place of the law courts. Two other important planks were Hindu-Moslem unity and the removal of untouchability among the Hindus.

The Congress also changed its constitution and became a body capable of action, and at the same time it laid itself out for a mass membership.

Now, this programme was a totally different thing from what the Congress had so afar been doing; indeed, it was quite a novel thing in the world, for the *Satyagraha* in South Africa had been very limited in its scope. It meant immediate and heavy sacrifices for some people, like the lawyers, who were called upon to give up their practices, and the students, who were asked to boycott the government colleges. It was difficult to judge it, as there were no standards of comparison. It is not surprising that the old and experienced Congress leaders hesitated and were filled with doubt. The greatest of them, Lokamanya Tilak, had died a little before this. Of the other prominent Congress leaders only one, Motilal Nehru, supported Gandhiji in the early stages. But there was no doubting the temper of the average Congressman, or the man in the street, or the masses. Gandhiji carried them off their feet, almost hypnotized them, and with loud shouts of *Mahatma Gandhi ki jai*, they showed their approval of the new gospel of non-violent non-cooperation. The Moslems were as enthusiastic about it as the others. Indeed, the Khilafat Committee, under the leadership of the Ali Brothers, had adopted the programme even before the

Congress did so. Soon the mass enthusiasm and the early successes of the movement brought most of the old Congress leaders into it. . . .

The Growth of Nationalism

The growth of nationalism turned people's minds to the necessity for political freedom. Freedom was necessary not only because it was degrading to be dependent and enslaved, not only because, as Tilak had put it, it was our birthright and we must have it, but also to lessen the burden of poverty from our people. How was freedom to be obtained? Obviously, we were not going to get it by remaining quiet and waiting for it. It was equally clear that methods of mere protest and begging, which the Congress had so far followed with more or less vehemence, were not only undignified for a people, but were also futile and ineffective. Never in history had such methods succeeded or induced a ruling or privileged class to part with power. History, indeed, showed us that peoples and classes who were enslaved had won their freedom through violent rebellion and insurrection.

Armed rebellion seemed out of the question for the Indian people. We were disarmed, and most of us did not even know the use of arms. Besides, in a contest of violence, the organized power of the British Government, or any state, was far greater than anything that could be raised against it. Armies might mutiny, but unarmed people could not rebel and face armed forces. Individual terrorism, on the other hand, the killing by bomb or pistol of individual terrorism, on the other hand, the killing by bomb or pistol of individual officers, was a bankrupt's creed. It was demoralizing for the people, and it was ridiculous to think that it could shake a powerfully organized government, however, much it might frighten individuals.

So all these avenues led nowhere, and there seemed to be no way out of the intolerable conditions of a degrading servitude. People who were at all sensitive felt terribly depressed and helpless. This was the moment when Gandhiji put forward his programme of non-cooperation. Like Sinn Fein in Ireland, it taught us to rely on ourselves and build up our own strength, and it was obviously a very effective method of bringing pressure on the government. The government rested very largely on the cooperation, willing or unwilling, of Indian themselves, and if this cooperation were withdrawn and the boycotts practised, it was quite possible, in theory, to bring down the whole structure of government.

Even if the non-cooperation did not go so far, there was no doubt that it could exert tremendous pressure on the government, and at the same time increase the strength of the people. It was to be perfectly peaceful, and yet it was not mere non-resistance. *Satyagraha* was a definite, though non-violent, form of resistance to what was considered wrong. It was, in effect, a peaceful rebellion, a most civilized form of warfare, and yet dangerous to the stability of the state. It was an effective way of getting the masses to function, and it seemed to fit in with the peculiar genius of the Indian people. It put us on our best behaviour and seemed to put the adversary in the wrong. It made us shed the fear that crushed us, and we began to look people in the face as we had never done before, and to speak out our minds fully and frankly. A great weight seemed to be lifted from our minds, and this new freedom of speech and action filled us with confidence and strength. And, finally, the method of peace prevented to a large extent the growth of those terribly bitter racial and national hatreds which had always so far accompanied such struggles, and thus made the ultimate settlement easier.

It is not surprising, therefore, that this programme of non-cooperation, coupled with the remarkable personality of Gandhiji, caught the imagination of the country and filled it with hope. It spread, and at its approach the old demoralization vanished. The new Congress attracted most of the vital elements in the country and grew in power and prestige.

The End of Fear

Not for a few years of excitement and agony and suspense, but for long generations our people had offered their 'blood, toil, sweat and tears'. And this process had eaten its way deep into the body and soul of India, poisoning every aspect of our corporate life, like that fell disease which consumes the tissues of the lungs and kills slowly but inevitably. Sometimes we thought that some swifter and more obvious process, resembling cholera or the bubonic plague, would have been better. But that was a passing thought, for adventurism leads nowhere, and the quack treatment of deep-seated diseases does not yield results.

And then Gandhiji came. He was like a powerful current of fresh air that made us stretch ourselves and take deep breaths, like a beam of light that pierced the darkness and removed the scales from our eyes, like a whirlwind that upset many things but most of all the working of people's minds. He did not descend from the top; he seemed to emerge from the millions of India, speaking their language and incessantly drawing attention to them and their appalling condition. Get off the backs of these peasants and workers, he told us, and you who live by their exploitation; get rid of the system that produces this poverty and misery.

Political freedom took new shape then and acquired a new content. Much that he said we only partially accepted or sometimes did not accept at all. But all this was secondary.

The essence of his teaching was fearlessness and truth and action allied to these, always, keeping the welfare of the masses in view. The greatest gift for an individual or a nation, so we had been told in our ancient books, was *abhaya,* fearlessness, not merely bodily courage but the absence of fear from the mind. Chanakya and Yagnavalkya had said, at the dawn of our history, that it was the function of the leaders of a people to make them fearless. But the dominant impulse in India under British rule was that of fear, pervasive, oppressing, strangling fear; fear of the army, the police, the widespread secret service; fear of the official class; fear of laws meant to suppress, and of prison; fear of the landlord's agent; fear of the moneylender; fear of unemployment and starvation, which were always on the threshold. It was against this all-pervading fear that Gandhiji's quiet and determined voice was raised. Be not afraid.

Was it so simple as all that? Not quite. And yet fear builds its phantoms which are more fearsome than reality itself, and reality when calmly analysed and its consequences willingly accepted loses much of its terror.

So, suddenly as it were, that black pall of fear was lifted from the people's shoulders, not wholly, of course, but to an amazing degree. As fear is close companion to falsehood, so truth follows fearlessness. The Indian people did not become much more truthful than they were, nor did they change their essential nature overnight, nevertheless a sea change was visible as the need for falsehood and furtive behaviour lessened. It was a psychological change, almost as if some expert in psychoanalytical method had probed deep into the patient's past, found out the origins of his complexes, exposed them to his view, and thus rid him of that burden.

There was that psychological reaction also, a feeling of shame at our long submission to an alien rule that had degraded and humiliated us, and a desire to submit no longer, whatever the consequences might be. We did not grow much more truthful, perhaps, than we had been previously, but Gandhiji was always there as a symbol of uncompromising truth to pull us up and shame us into truth.

Gandhiji and Truth

What is truth? I do not know for certain, and perhaps our truths are relative and absolute truth is beyond us. Different persons may and do take different views of truth, and each individual is powerfully influenced by his own background, training, and impulses. So also Gandhiji. But truth is at least for an individual what he himself feels and knows to be true. According to that definition I do not know of any person who holds to the truth as Gandhiji does. That is a dangerous quality in a politician, for he speaks out his mind and even lets the public see its changing phases.

Gandhiji influenced millions of people in India in varying degrees; some changed the whole texture of their lives, others were only partly affected, or the effect wore off, and yet not quite, for some part of it could not be wholly shaken off. Different people reacted differently, and each will give his own answer to this question. Some might well say almost in the words of Alcibiades.

Besides, when we listen to any one else talking, however, eloquent he is, we don't really care a damn what he says; but when we listen to you, or to someone else repeating what you've said, even if he puts it ever so badly, and never mind whether the person who is listening is man, woman, or child, we're absolutely staggered and bewitched and speaking for myself, gentlemen, if I wasn't afraid you'd tell me I was completely bottled, I'd swear on oath what an extraordinary effect his words have had on me—and still do, if it comes to that. For the moment I hear him speak I am smitten by a kind of sacred rage, worse than any Corybant, and my heart jumps into my mouth and the tears start into my eyes—Oh, and not only me, but lots of other men.

Yes, I have heard Pericles and all the other great orators, and very eloquent I thought they were; but they never affected me like that; they never turned my whole soul upside down and left me feeling as if I were the lowest of the low; but this latter day Maryas, here, has often left me in such a state of mind that I've felt I simply couldn't go on living the way I did. . . .

And there is one thing I've never felt with anybody else—not the kind of thing you would expect to find in me, either—and that is a sense of shame. Socrates is the only man in the world that can make me feel ashamed. Because there's no getting away from it, I know I ought to do the things he tells me to, and yet the moment I'm out of his sight I don't care what I do to keep in with the mob. So I dash off like a runaway slave, a keep out of his way as long as I can and then next time I meet him I remember all that I had to admit the time before, and naturally I feel ashamed. . . .

Only I've been bitten by something much more poisonous than a snake, in fact, mine is the most painful kind of bite there is I've been bitten in the heart, or the mind, or whatever you like to call it.

Gandhiji Makes Congress a Mass Orgnization

Gandhiji for the first time entered the Congress organization and immediately brought about a complete change in its constitution. He made it democratic and a mass organization. Democratic it had been previously also, but it had so far been limited in franchise and restricted to the upper classes. Now the peasants rolled in, and in its new garb it began to assume the look of a vat agrarian organization with a strong sprinkling of the middle classes. This agrarian character was to grow. Industrial workers also came in, but as individuals and not in their separate, organized capacity.

Action was to be the basis and objective of this roganization, action based on peaceful methods. Thus far the alterntives had been: just talking and passing resolutions, or terroristic activity. Both of the these were set aside, and terrorism was especially condemned as opposed to the basic policy of the Congress. A new technique of action was evolved which, though perfectly peaceful, yet involved non-submission to what was considered wrong, and as a consequence, a willing acceptance of the pain and suffering involved in this. Gandhiji was an odd kind of pacifist, for he was an activist full of dynamic energy. There was no submission in him to fate or anything that he considered evil, he was full of resistance, though this was peaceful and courteous.

The call of action was twofold. There was of course the action involved in challenging and resisting foreign rulers, there was also the action which led us to fight our own social evils. Apart from the fundamental objective of the Congress—the freedom of India—and the method of peaceful action, the principal planks of the Congress were national unity, which involved the solution of the minority problems, and the raising of the depressed classes and the ending of the curse of untouchability.

The New Ideology

Realizing that the main props of British rule were fear, prestige, the cooperation, willing or unwilling, of the people, and certain classes whose vested interests were centred in

British rule, Gandhiji attacked these foundations. Titles were to be given up, and though the title holders responded to this only in a small measure, the popular respect for these British-given titles disappeared and they became symbols of degradation. New standards and values were set up, and the pomp and splendour of the viceregal court and princes, which used to impress so much, suddenly appeared supremely ridiculous and vulgar and rather shameful, surrounded as they were by the poverty and misery of the people. Rich men were not so anxious to flaunt their riches; outwardly at least many of them adopted simpler ways, and in their dress became almost indistinguishable from humbler folk.

The older leaders of the Congress, nurtured in a different and more quiescent tradition, did not take easily to these new ways and were disturbed by the upsurge of the masses. Yet so powerful was the wave of feeling and sentiment that swept through the country that some of that intoxication filled them also. A very few fell away, and among them was Mr. M.A. Jinnah. He left the Congress not because of any difference of opinion on the Hindu-Moslem question but because he could not adapt himself to the new and more advanced ideology, and even more because he disliked the crowds of ill-dressed people, talking in Hindustani, who filled the Congress. His idea of politics was of a superior variety, more suited to the legislative chamber or to a committee room. For some years he felt completely out of the picture and even decided to leave India for good. He settled down in England and spent several years there.

It is said, and I think with truth, that the Indian habit of mind is essentially one of quietism. Perhaps old races develop that attitude to life; a long tradition of philosophy also leads to it. And yet Gandhiji, a typical product of India, represents the very antithesis of quietism. He has been a demon of energy and action, a hustler, and a man who not only drives himself but drives others. He has done more than anyone I know to fight and change the quiet of the Indian people.

He sent us to the villages, and the countryside hummed with the activity of innumerable messengers of the new gospel of action. The peasant was shaken up and he began to emerge from his quiescent shell. The effect on us was different but equally far-reaching, for we saw, for the first time as it were, the villager in the intimacy of his mud hut and with the stark shadow of hunger always pursuing him. We learned our Indian economics more from these visits than from books and learned discourses. The emotional experience we had already undergone was emphasized and confirmed, and henceforward there could be no going back for us to our old life or our old standards, howsoever much our views might change subsequently.

Gandhiji held strong views on economic, social, and other matters. He did not try to impose all of these on the Congress, though he continued to develop his ideas, and sometimes in the process varied them, through his writings. But some he tried to push into the Congress. He proceeded cautiously, for he wanted to carry the people with him. Sometimes he went too far for the Congress and had to retrace his steps. Not many accepted his views in their entirety; some disagreed with that fundamental outlook. But many accepted them in the modified form in which they came to the Congress as being suited to the circumstances then existing. In two respects the background of his thoughts had a vague but considerable influence: the fundamental test of everything was how far it benefited the masses, and the means were always important and could not be ignored even though the end in view was right, for the means governed the end and varied it.

A Hindu without any Dogma

Gandhiji was essentially a man of religion, a Hindu to the innermost depths of his being, and yet his conception of religion had nothing to do with any dogma or custom or ritual. It was basically concerned with his firm belief in the moral law, which he calls the law of Truth or Love. Truth and non-violence appear to him to be the same thing or different aspects of one and the same thing, and he uses these words almost interchangeably.

Claiming to understand the spirit of Hinduism, he rejects every text or practice which does not fit in with his idealist interpretation of what it should be, calling it an interpolation or a subsequent accretion. 'I decline to be a slave', he has said, 'to precedents or practices I cannot understand or defend on a moral basis'. And so in practice he is singularly free to take the path of his choice, to change and adapt himself, to develop his philosophy of life and action, subject only to the overriding consideration of the moral law as he conceives this to be. Whether that philosophy is right or wrong may be argued, but he insists on applying the same fundamental yardstick to everything, and himself specially. In politics, as in other aspects of life, this creates difficulties for the average person, and often misunderstanding. But no difficulty makes him swerve from the straight line of his choosing, though within limits he is continually adapting himself to a changing situation. Every reform that he suggests, every advice that he gives to others, he straightway applies to himself. He is always beginning with himself, and his words and actions fit into each other like a glove on the hand. And so, whatever happens, he never loses his integrity and there is always an organic completeness about his life and work. Even in his apparent failures he has seemed to grow in stature.

What was his idea of India which he was setting out to mould according to his own wishes and ideals? 'I shall work for an India in which the poorest shall feel that it is their country, in whose making they have an effective voice, an India in which there shall be no high class and low class of people, an India in which all communities shall live in perfect harmony. There can be no room in such an India for the curse of untouchability, for the curse of intoxicating drinks and drugs. . . . Women who will enjoy the same rights as men. . . . This is the India of my dreams.'

Proud of his Hindu inheritance as he was, he tried to give to Hinduism a kind of universal attire and included all religions within the fold of truth. He refused to narrow his cultural inheritance. 'Indian culture', he wrote, 'is neither Hindu, Islamic nor any other, wholly. It is a fusion of all'. Again he said: 'I want the culture of all lands to be blown about my house as freely as possible. But I refuse to be blown off my feet by any. I refuse to live in other people's houses as an interloper, a beggar or a slave'. Influenced by modern thought currents, he never let go of his roots and clung to them tenaciously.

Spiritual Unity

And so he set about to restore the spiritual unity of the people and to break the barrier between the small westernized group at the top and the masses, to discover the living elements in the old roots and to build upon them, to waken in these masses, out of their stupor and static condition and make them dynamic. In his single-track and yet many-sided nature the dominating impression that one gathered was his identification with the masses, a community of spirit with them, an amazing sense of unity with the dispossessed and poverty-stricken not only of India but of the world. Even religion, as everything else, took second place to his passion to raise these submerged people. 'A semi-starved nation can have neither religion nor art nor organization.' 'Whatever can be useful to starving millions is beautiful to my mind. Let us give today first the vital things of life, and all the graces and ornaments of life will follow. . . . I want art and literature that can speak to millions'. These unhappy dispossessed millions haunted him, and everything seemed to revolve round them. 'For millions it is an eternal vigil or an eternal trance.' His ambition, he said, was to 'wipe every tear from every eye'.

It is not surprising that this astonishingly vital man, full of self-confidence and an unusual kind of power, standing for equality and freedom for each individual, but measuring all this in terms of the poorest, fascinated the masses of India and attracted them like a magnet. He seemed to them to link up the past with the future and to make the dismal present appear just as a stepping-stone to that future of life and hope. And not the masses only, but intellectuals, and others also, though their minds were often troubled and confused and the change-over for them from the habits of lifetimes was more difficult. Thus he effected a vast psychological revolution not only among those who followed his lead but also among his opponents and those many neutrals who could not make up their minds what to think and what to do.

Congress was dominated by Gandhiji, and yet it was a peculiar domination, for the Congress was an active, rebellious, many-sided organization, full of a variety of opinion, and not easily led this way or that. Often Gandhiji toned down his position to meet the wishes of others, sometimes he accepted even an adverse decision. On some vital matters for him he was adamant, and on more than one occasion there came a break between him and the Congress. But

always he was the symbol of India's independence and militant nationalism, the unyielding opponent of all those who sought to enslave her, and it was as such a symbol that people gathered to him and accepted his lead, even though they disagreed with him on other matters. They did not always accept that lead when there was no active struggle going on, but when the struggle was inevitable, that symbol became all-important and everything else was secondary.

A Bourgeois Movement

It should be remembered that the nationalist movement in India, like all nationalist movements, was essentially a bourgeois movement. It represented the natural historical stage of development, and to consider it or to characterise it as a working-class movement is wrong. Gandhiji represented that movement and the Indian masses in relation to that movement to a supreme degree, and he became the voice of the Indian people to that extent. He functioned inevitably within the orbit of nationalist ideology, but the dominating passion that consumed him was a desire to raise the masses. In this respect he was always ahead of the nationalist movement, and he gradually made it, within the limits of its own ideology, turn in this direction. Economic events in India and the world powerfully pushed Indian nationalism towards vital social changes, and today it hovers, somewhat undecided, on the brink of a new social ideology.

But the main contribution of Gandhiji to India and the Indian masses has been through the powerful movements which he launched through the National Congress. Through nation-wide action he sought to mould the millions, and largely succeeded in doing so, and changing them from a demoralized, timid, and incapable of resistance into a people

with self-respect and self-reliance, resisting tyranny, and capable of united action and sacrifice for a larger cause. He made them think of political and economic issues, and every village and every bazaar hummed with argument and debate on the new ideas and hopes that filled the people. That was an amazing psychological change. The time was ripe for it, of course, and circumstances and world conditions worked for this change. But a great leader is necessary to take advantage of circumstances and conditions. Gandhiji was that leader, and he released many of the bonds that imprisoned and disabled our minds, and none of us who experienced it can ever forget that great feeling of release and exhilaration that came over the Indian people. Gandhiji has played a revolutionary role in India of the greatest importance because he knew how to make the most of the objective conditions and could reach the heart of the masses; while groups with a more advanced ideology functioned largely in the air because they did not fit in with those conditions and could therefore not evoke any substantial response from the masses. . . .

Raising the Masses

It is perfectly true that Gandhiji, functioning in the nationalist plane, does not think in terms of the conflict of classes, and tries to compose their differences. But the action he has indulged in and taught the people has inevitably raised mass consciousness tremendously and made social issues vital. And his insistence on the raising of the masses at the cost, wherever necessary, of vested interests has given a strong orientation to the national movement in favour of the masses.

Essentially, the Congress under Gandhiji's leadership has been a joint and anti-imperialist front.

Gandhiji and the Congress must be judged by the policies

they pursue and the action they indulge in. But behind this, personality counts and colours those policies and activities. In the case of a very exceptional person like Gandhiji the question of personality becomes especially important in order to understand and appraise him. An English journalist, Mr. George Slocombe, who has had a wide experience of men prominent and otherwise in public affairs all over the world, has referred to Gandhiji in a recent book of his, and the passage is interesting and worth quoting. He says: 'I have never met any man more utterly honest, more transparently sincere, less given to egotism, self-conscious pride, opportunism, and ambition which are found in greater or less degree in all the other great political figures of the world.' An English journalist's opinion need not carry much weight with us, nor does the sincerity of a person excuse a wrong policy or mistaken ideas. But as it happens, that opinion is shared by millions in India, and it is very superficial criticism to dispose of such a unique and outstanding personality by cheap and well-worn phrases which are applied indiscriminately to the average politician. We in India have often differed from Gandhiji, we differ from him still in many ways, and sometimes we may follow different paths, but it has been the greatest privilege of our lives to work with him and under him for a great cause. To us he has represented the spirit and honour of India, the yearning of her sorrowing millions to be rid of their innumerable burdens, and an insult to him by the British government or others has been an insult to India and her people.

World Federation

Gandhiji gave a turn to our nationalist movement which lessened the feelings of frustration and bitterness. Those feelings continued, but I do not know of any other nationalist movement which has been so free from hatred. Gandhiji was an intense nationalist; he was also, at the same time, a man who felt he had a message not only for India but for the world, and he ardently desired world peace. His nationalism, therefore, had a certain world outlook and was entirely free from any aggressive intent. Desiring the independence of India, he had come to believe that a world federation of interdependent states was the only right goal, however distant that might be. He had said: 'My idea of nationalism is that my country may become free, that if need be the whole of the country may die, so that the human race may live. There is no room for race hatred here. Let that be our nationalism'. And again: 'I do want to think in terms of the whole world. My patriotism includes the good of mankind in general. Therefore, my service of India includes the service of humanity. . . . Isolated independence is not the goal of the world states. It is voluntary interdependence. The better mind of the world desires today not absolutely independent states, warring one against another, but a federation of friendly, interdependent states. The consummation of that event may be far off. I want to make no grand claim for our country. But I see nothing grand or impossible about our expressing our readiness for universal interdependence rather than independence. I desire the ability to be totally independent without asserting the independence.'

Index